The

Blessings

Paul
Butler

The Little Book of Annoying Questions

Understanding the Coming New American Revolution and an Unexpected Generation

Phill Bettis

CROSSBOOKS
PUBLISHING

CrossBooks™
A Division of LifeWay
1663 Liberty Drive
Bloomington, IN 47403
www.crossbooks.com
Phone: 1-866-879-0502

First published by CrossBooks 7/5/2012

ISBN: 978-1-4627-1912-9 (sc)
ISBN: 978-1-4627-1913-6 (e)
ISBN: 978-1-4627-1974-7 (hc)
All references to Bible quotes are to the King James Version with one
reference on Page 46 to the New King James Version

Printed in the United States of America

This book is printed on acid-free paper.

Any people depicted in stock imagery provided by Thinkstock are models,
and such images are being used for illustrative purposes only.

Certain stock imagery © Thinkstock.

For God the Father, Son, and Holy Spirit; and for Wanda, Emily, Barry, Spenser, Mom and Dad, and grandparents long gone: Leland, Harold, Charles, Frank, John, and Lois.

If my people, which are called by my name, shall humble themselves, and pray, and seek my face, and turn from their wicked ways; then will I hear from heaven, and will forgive their sin, and will heal their land.

2 Chronicles 7:14

Contents

Preface

December 26, 2011, began gray and chilly. Noting the rare occurrence of hoarfrost on the rooftop of my North Georgia home, I considered the proper usage of the day after Christmas. My twentysomething children were home from school for a few days, fully reloaded with some cash and gift cards and ready for a day at the mall. I relish time spent with them, but my weariness with shopping and eating was evident. I needed some exercise and some time alone. A long walk in chilled winter air would help clear the fog of the holidays.

December 26 was, at one time in my life, a very sad day. The sudden end of church and family events, great meals, and brightly lit decorations hit hard. As I matured, as family members went home to be with the Lord, and as my own family grew, I eventually realized that every day is a blessing. The passing of Christmas reminds us of a persistent but very blessed march toward our destinies. The holidays also provide time to take stock, to prepare for another year, and to hope for better. I can't help reminiscing, too. My grown children were at one time wearing footie pajamas and excited about a rocking horse or a cowboy hat. Gift cards and sweaters are just not quite the same. I do enjoy wonderful children who look forward to their time at home and who, despite their age, still love Christmas morning. I wondered if

Christmas morning is a glimpse into eternity, an eternity where we all rejoice at being together, where struggles will be long forgotten, where money means nothing, and where joy is the order of the day.

With so many holiday events and family gatherings, the time to focus entirely on my family was limited to a brief hour or two on Christmas morning. It is not at all surprising that we lose some perspective and focus during the holidays. Walking long distances alone allows thought, prayer, and an opportunity to become closer to God. Recently my prayers and relationship with God have become much more intimate. Like a child returning home for the holidays, I returned to my Father's house to be fed and nurtured, to be loved, encouraged, and inspired. I have little doubt that our heavenly Father rejoices when we return home. He provides gifts of peace, joy, and understanding with such loving generosity that we cannot help being overwhelmed. Sharing this journey with two very close friends at a holiday meal, it became apparent that God was working in their lives too. Both were at peace and inspired to serve God like never before. One had suffered extreme health problems; the other had suffered extreme financial problems due to the recent recession. I was impressed with their drive to serve God more willingly, more deeply, and more sacrificially. Their studies had become more intense, and missions into communities and lives yet untouched became more important. I relate these accounts for one reason. God is working among us in incredibly powerful methods in preparation for events so wonderful, so amazing, and so profound that even the faithful will be surprised. No, I don't think the world is ending in 2012 as the movies and the Maya predict. I do think we are on the precipice of a "coming home" event where God's love for us and our love for him will explode on the world scene, a world that has done almost everything to write off our heavenly Father.

My favorite walking route is along a trail built beside a small tributary of the Chattahoochee River named Big Creek. Expecting to be alone with my thoughts and prayers on the day after Christmas, I was surprised to find runners and families with small children sharing the trail early in the morning. Gone were the summer months when the trail was extremely busy with bicyclists, runners, and walkers like me. Recent rains had filled wetlands surrounding Big Creek, where heaps of acorns accumulated from rainwater scouring the woods. Squirrels and ducks in search of scarce winter sustenance had yet to discover the cache. A large man wearing a Georgia Tech hoodie ran, gasping for breath, unaware of anyone or anything but his struggle to take the next step and breathe. I wondered if that man was symbolic of so many of us. He was trying mightily to do what was expected—be in shape, thin down, be disciplined—all the while expending great effort, experiencing great pain, and likely being oblivious to any needs other than his own. Was he a snapshot of twenty-first-century America?

Walking and listening to my iPod, my thoughts rushed by like those creeks and eddies filling a long-dry swamp. Work, family, and nature all came to mind, at least until there was only God on a now beautiful morning among pines, river birch, and oaks lining the trail. Despite having walked this trail many, many times over the last year, I was for some reason reminded this time of a story once shared by my grandfather. My home is constructed on his small farm, and my life is constructed on many of his principles, stories, and teachings. Grandfather lost his father at age three. Without help from neighbors, his young mother would have struggled to just put food on the table. Living in a South still reeling from the miserable effects of the Civil War and Reconstruction, a South where agriculture ruled and where single mothers struggled to provide for their families with meager crops, Grandfather was nevertheless allowed a rather rambunctious childhood.

The story shared by my grandfather took place only a few steps from my walking path. Over one hundred years ago, when my grandfather was a preteen, he and other boys became curious about a sand-dredging machine floating down Big Creek. Swimming too closely, he was pulled underwater by the strong suction of the dredging machine. In his later years, Grandfather told this story with the clear purpose of warning me about swimming too closely to anything that would suck me in. I clearly understood his admonition about curiosity and recklessness and about temptations that drown us in addictions, obsessions, and wrong decisions. I loved that man as much as any living soul in my life. He was simple, opinionated, hard-working, and, indeed, thankful to have a life that came close to being extinguished at a young age.

Remembering Grandfather's story, I realized that my destiny, my existence, could have ended with a simple childhood indiscretion. Our existence is held together by the thinnest of threads yet is nevertheless, thankfully, governed by God's destiny and plan for each one of us.

Other stories emanate from the swamps surrounding Big Creek. Here rabbits half as long as a man would become dinner for boys armed with .22 rifles. Snakes were always venomous and, when stretched by distant memory, "as big as stovepipes." Boys, including my father, would seine (fish with a net), catching fish and water moccasins alike. Braver boys would blindly reach well into crevices located along creek banks hoping that snakes and snapping turtles were lenient. As far as I know, everyone survived with fingers intact and without snake bites. Those adventurers lived long enough to fight in the World Wars and return to marry, rear children, serve in their churches, retire, and struggle with aging. Stories of Big Creek Swamp are freely told, rightfully embellished, and endlessly fascinating. Each one of those men, including my grandfather and father, possessed a destiny. And their destiny was and is inextricably connected to mine. All of our lives are connected to the destinies of our families, our churches, our schools, and our nation. Whether we like one another or not, our good and bad decisions affect one another. There is no doubt a social and economic cost to our decisions.

Nations have destinies too. Many believe our nation peaked in the 1950s or early 1960s. Some comment that 9/11 ended the American Century and that we must now give way to the economies of China, India, and other emerging nations. Financial responsibility, or lack thereof, troubles us. Many of the world's governments fear citizen reaction when social programs can no longer be funded. No nation or individual on Earth can in perpetuity spend more than is taken in. Do we trust history's revelation that few nations, especially republics, survive more than two or three centuries? Is that because lifestyle becomes more valuable than liberty? Are many seeking security only to inherit what Churchill described as "shared misery?" *Do we really believe that America is somehow exempt from the aftermath of poor stewardship? Do we have a destiny of prosperity and blessings regardless of our actions and beliefs?* Are we swimming behind the sand dredge? Are we approaching a "near death" experience as a nation? Will we live to tell the tales? Will we warn others?

Mark Twain once wrote something to the effect that the news of his death had been greatly exaggerated. The reports of our national demise and our spiritual death have also been greatly exaggerated. No doubt, we have problems. So did our ancestors. Inexplicably, we remain a great nation. Explicably, we remain for a reason. I encounter many people who truly believe we are done for as a nation, that we should be storing food, supplies, and weapons and otherwise planning an exit strategy. Those naysayers are missing something, though. Young people who are similar in age to my children, those "twentysomethings," are coming off the assembly line of good homes (or the rejection of bad homes), godly influence, and extensive education armed with a revolutionary spirit unlike any generation existent since our founding fathers. Those young adults are keenly aware of health care votes, budget deficits, job statistics, external threats, and concerns about our morality and direction. Oddly, they have reversed the long-standing tradition of older generations worrying about those that follow and are instead worried about current squandering, self-absorption, lack of discipline, and the declining educational and degraded business environments, all fostered by the generation in charge. The next generation is rightfully angry and disgusted and will not be ignored. In a season of Occupy Movements and Arab Springs, how will this clearly different group of young people emerge and react? Such is the purpose of this brief writing: to encourage a much-needed and anticipated wave of reformation and renewal benefiting a nation thirsty for some credible sources of vision and strength. Add to that thirst the reemergence of truth, personal responsibility, and freedom, and the resulting brew is toxic to those who believe that our best days are long gone. God is working among an elect and chosen group of young people to reclaim a nation that remains the best hope for sharing the gospel and leading the world.

I understand this writing will be controversial. I am a suburban real estate lawyer. I have experienced an interesting life and been richly blessed, but some of the questions posed in this book gave pause. God's strong call to share this writing left me constantly wondering, *Why me?* Why would God call someone to write about what so many of us are thinking? Was this writing part of my destiny? Was I swimming behind the sand dredge? Did I trust God's call in my life? Did I listen when he offered reassurance and confirmation? Did I trust that he would take care of me while inspiring and guiding me?

Obviously, I prayed about this writing, and on one of those prayerful days, God impressed me to visit my earthly father's house.

My earthly father, whom I call Dad, suffers along with my mom from severe dementia. He is also blind. Surgery last year left him in a steadily declining physical and mental condition, and at age eighty-seven, there is not much to be done but make sure he is comfortable. Seeing someone who lived out those stories along Big Creek and who led a good life as a builder and deacon and in service to his community suffer the indignities of age and sickness is not easy. Conversations often consist of little more than a light hug and "How are you today?"

Arriving at his home and without a word being said, Dad immediately knew who I was. His once strong hand reached for mine and applied a familiar and firm grip. His caretaker began to share how Dad had been praying since early that morning. He began again as we held hands. "God will do what he said he would do!" Dad repeated this statement several times, becoming more emotional as he did so. Through a seriously impaired man, a man whom I love, my heavenly Father sent the reassurance I sought. Why *not* me?

This writing took place on family vacations, early in the morning, and late at night. Sticky notes littered my desk and bathroom mirror to remind me of thoughts or concerns. I realized that no one wants to read several hundred pages of dark concerns and suggested corrections, but organizing a torrent of thoughts that had accumulated over many years into a purposely short writing was a challenge.

The use of questions throughout this writing forces readers to confront issues. Some of those issues are personal, and some are societal. Some questions will seem trivial; some questions may never have an answer. Confronting long-ignored issues forces an end to denial, increases awareness, and annoys the stuffing out of us. There is also a risk of being overwhelmed, and being overwhelmed can quickly lead to resignation. But resignation is not an option for the emerging leaders who will be illuminated and explored in this writing. No doubt questions will arise about these leaders. New leaders always displace others, and those displaced or challenged will feel left out. And being left out can lead to intense dissension. Others will ask, "Where are we headed?" and "Are we there yet?" Aren't those questions we were asking anyway?

This writing is not meant to be scary. Quite the contrary, I hope and pray to share insight that renewal does not mean destruction and that new ideas are not necessarily bad or threatening. Despite all of our differences, we do at least share one condition. That shared condition exists regardless of wealth, education, color, and beliefs. That condition is simply our destinies.

Acknowledgments

I wish to thank the following individuals who edited and encouraged me as this book was being written and long before: Barry, Cleve, Emily, Linda, Ian, Lindsay, Kyle, Pam, Samantha, Kay, Ken and family, Clifton, and Dr. Werner, and former teachers and professors Dr. Bryant, Mrs. Tiller, Mrs. Ledbetter, and Ms. Anderson.

CHAPTER 1

One Question, Please?

No question is so difficult to answer as that
to which the answer is obvious.
—George Bernard Shaw

I love to travel, and you will quickly note that any invitation to travel short of a root canal junket will find me eagerly packing. When a young lawyer in my office recently invited the "old guy" to accompany him for a private tour of the Pentagon, I immediately accepted. My first trip to Washington, DC occurred in 1981, a year when our economy was troubled and our international prestige had been dinged not only by the outcome of the Vietnam War but also by the Iran hostage crisis. Jimmy Carter's defeat in 1980 allowed for a much-needed change in leadership style embodied in Ronald Reagan. In 1981, my marriage and law practice were both new, and I couldn't help being excited about what God had in store for my life. That excitement was not always shared. Older lawyers, both in my practice and in court, often bemoaned a lack of national productivity, rampant immorality, and a still struggling economy. Some even believed that the economy would never recover in their lifetimes. Very few in my circle of friends and colleagues believed an American renaissance was imminent. Who in their right mind would have dreamed that a quarter century of prosperity would soon follow, as would many wars, terrorist attacks, and innovations? Before computers were personal, before iPods and iPads; before "the cloud"; before e-mail, eBay, and Facebook, there were dreams dreamed in backyards, makeshift laboratories, and garages all across the nation. In 1981, many of those dreamers and doers were young, ambitious, and committed to changing the world. They did.

Fast-forward thirty years. Somewhere along the way, I became just like those old lawyers present in my early practice years; I had assumed the unrighteous role of a pessimist. There were many, many reasons that role should never have been taken on. My children were grown, smart, and spiritual, and my marriage and home were blessed and intact. Yet negativity became low-hanging fruit to be consumed, not with relish but with plenty of company. Oh, I had my reasons. An out-of-control and out-of-touch Congress frustrated me to no end. I felt that no vote, no voice, and no protest would ever change that unholy gathering. The collapse of the economy hit my business especially hard. As a real estate lawyer in an Atlanta suburb, I had never lacked for business, but in 2007, my closing practice virtually disintegrated before my eyes. With kids in college and overhead that never ended, I had a serious problem on my hands. At the same time, my heart was burdened as never before for so many people living without any spiritual influence whatsoever in their lives. That lack of influence began showing up in daily news reports, broken homes, addictions, and so many other situations that crept into my life via daily phone messages and e-mails. Church attendance had declined, Christian influence was waning, and the only response seemed to be more covered-dish dinners and a resignation that Jesus would soon return and take everyone out of their misery. Yes, I got down. My descent to virtual despair was precipitous and complete. Understand that when we hit rock bottom, when nothing in the world seems to be working, God does.

God reminded me of an eager young lawyer who was at one time anxious to embrace the future, regardless of what the pessimists thought. Pulling me from a dark place, God also reminded me that my children were nearing the end of their college and graduate studies, looking for jobs, and dreaming of their own families. Was it not their turn? My children are not at all negative about the future, and neither are their friends. They may be concerned, but those young adults have not given up at all. Weddings still occur, degrees are conferred, careers launched, babies born, new cars and houses bought, and dreams pursued. Some of those dreams occur in backyards, makeshift laboratories, and garages. Some of those dreams will change the world again.

God also used the good sense of my gentle wife, who forbade my absorption of news and talk shows until I could get my "head on straight." (There may be some debate in her mind if that is ever really possible.) Her advice allowed perspective and was in no way intended to deny that our nation and people have some serious issues. When I needed more perspective, her suggestion to resume volunteer work at a local food bank was most appropriate. Our visits there quickly reminded me that I had no real reason to offer any complaint or to be down and out. She also encouraged my trip to Washington, DC, knowing that a good trip would clear my head and heart.

Arriving at Reagan National Airport, we quickly unloaded our luggage, hailed a cab, and traveled to our hotel near Embassy Row in Washington, DC. A mad rush to see as much as possible found us on the Metro with a power tour of one of the Smithsonian museums squeezed in before our late-day visit to the Pentagon. When we got to the Pentagon, there was just enough time to view the recently completed 9/11 Pentagon Memorial. Remembering the loss of 184 lives at the

Pentagon, one as young as three and the oldest at seventy-one, was extremely moving. Few realize that about one fifth of the Pentagon was destroyed or severely affected by the impact of a terrorist-piloted aircraft. Entering the rebuilt portion of the Pentagon where the impact occurred, where lives were cut short in a matter of seconds, our tour group became silent and reflective. A decade of war and loss of young American soldiers touched my heart, a heart still occasionally very angry at terrorists and those filled with hatred, jealousy, and extremism. Yellow-tinted windows beaming late-day sunlight provided a cathedral-like air to a small room once filled with burning jet fuel but now dedicated to the memory of those lost on that fateful day. I wondered whether the flame of liberty was reignited here or those flames simply destroyed a way of life that existed before September 11, 2001.

Our tour concluded with a rare visit to the portion of the Pentagon where the Secretary of Defense and the Joint Chiefs maintain their offices. Decisions made in these offices separate families, end lives, and affect the whole world. A simple question came to mind.

Arising early the next morning, following a good night's rest, I was intent on absorbing every nuance of our nation's capital. Walking as the sun rose on a beautiful, cool fall morning, I was surprised at the serenity of Washington's streets. Perhaps everyone would arrive later; maybe they were all on the Metro or stuck in traffic. Was it simply too early?

My walk along 16th Street to the White House revealed building after building housing lobbyists and special interest groups. K Street is home to lobbyists advocating industries, teachers, animal and human rights, and, no doubt, foreign governments. As I walked by those buildings, realizing that those inside worked for a living just as I did, I wondered if lobbying simply exists for one group to have an advantage over another. Is it possible that our foundational belief in equality is now being offered for sale? For that matter, was this whole town for sale?

Were these lobbyists the modern-day equivalents to moneychangers at the temple? There was still that one nagging question, though—the same question that was on my heart at the Pentagon.

When I arrived at the White House, a location where gunshots had been fired earlier in the same week, I stood a moment in Lafayette Square, contemplating the memory of Lafayette and his contributions to our Revolutionary War victory. In odd honor to those hard-fought-for freedoms, protestors were camped at the edge of the park, showcasing their opposition to nuclear war. Assuming the role of an awestruck tourist, I snapped numerous photos. Washington was reluctantly awakening to face another day.

In the dim morning light, the White House seemed diminutive, fragile, and vulnerable. No doubt the West Wing was caffeinated, wide awake, and making grave decisions for a nation at war and suffering from a long and deep recession. My last time standing outside the White House gates occurred during a very humid July week, very much in contrast to a chilled November morning. Contrasts abounded as I considered how much had changed in the past thirty years for both my family and my nation. Were those changes for the better? Certainly my family had been blessed, as had my nation. But I worried about both. Would my children have the same opportunities I had experienced? Would recession and war become a way of life? Was our nation in decline or in pause before our best days? Why must we be so divided? Do we care about one another, or do those special interests so close by on K Street matter more? For the occupants of the White House and the West Wing, I had that same annoying question I had considered during my walk along 16th Street and at the Pentagon.

Searching for that little place where Washington eats breakfast, a place that exists in every large city and small town, I found that a bustling Starbucks was the likely candidate. I am sure there are other unique places, but hunger and the need for some human interaction made Starbucks my choice. Wedging myself in among young Washington office workers, I wondered where the adults were. The average age seemed to be twentysomething. Those young people were pleasant, courteous, and focused on getting to work. After my order was placed, an older man seemed anxious to engage in a moment of conversation. Incongruous with the well-dressed, younger diners surrounding us, we did talk briefly. I wondered if he was homeless, searching for a place of warmth and perhaps a warm word from someone. Glad to find one available small table, I thoroughly enjoyed a good cup of coffee, a breakfast sandwich, and the excitement of young Washingtonians anticipating the weekend that would soon follow. Thanksgiving week would follow that weekend, and plans were underway for travel, family reunions, and seeing old friends. Since my children are of similar age, I understood their hunger for staying in touch with friends, for new experiences, and for building resumes. A young lady smiled at me, perhaps recognizing someone similar to her father in an alien environment, perhaps having pity on someone as out of place as the homeless man in a young, vivacious world of hope and promise. I wondered while reading the day's headlines if anyone in this vibrant city—a city with a European feel, a city likely unaware of the pulse of the land beyond the borders of Starbucks, the Metro, or nearby Maryland and Virginia—had any idea of what was to come. My one question, posed earlier at the White House, had not gone away.

Not far away, Occupy Washington members were camped in parks with news crews paying a daily visit, while Occupy events in other cities occupied many news reports. Interview after interview revealed an agenda or, with some, a lack thereof. Corporate greed, capitalism, bailouts, and student loans were all topics of protest and debate, but those at home questioned who was behind these protesters, what was really going on, and whether at some point this movement would move to violence. I observed ragtag villages of tents and remembered Woodstock and massive protests occurring on the nearby Washington Mall during the 1960s. For those Occupy Washington participants spending cold nights outside, living in deplorable conditions, and hungering for attention, I had an annoying question to ask.

Without benefit of GPS or a compass, I continued my journey through what had clearly become morning rush hour. While constantly wondering if I had taken a wrong turn, and simultaneously relishing history and architecture, I would eventually reach the Mall well ahead of the Smithsonian openings. The Capitol building beckoned in the distance, and I obliged. Fall colors remained vibrant, especially among tulip trees lining the Capitol grounds. Fellow tourists converged, many with young children who effortlessly climbed step after step until confronted by stoic guards protecting the Capitol building from errant five-year-olds. Picturesque in the bright fall sunlight and surrounded by office buildings, news crews, and ever-present security, the Capitol was impressive, symbolic, and strangely quiet. Wishing for something better than my cell phone camera, I snapped photo after photo as I wound around the building, eventually observing the Supreme Court building on the east side of the Capitol building. As a lawyer, that building had special significance. Any lawyer worth his or her salt dreams of arguing a case in that building, and I am no exception. As I stood between buildings symbolizing two branches of our government, wondering if anyone there had a clue and why no one could discipline our national spending or pull us together, my one question reappeared.

An afternoon visit to the Smithsonian Air and Space Museum brought back memories of shade darkened school libraries where students intently watched the first American manned space launches by Scott Carpenter and John Glenn on grainy black and white television sets. Touching one of their Mercury space capsules, observing spacesuits worn by heroes and then the *Spirit of St. Louis*—Lindbergh's plane—warplanes, and rockets, I was overwhelmed. Visiting the Museum of American History followed, and I read almost every detail of almost every exhibit, a propensity that caused my wife to adamantly state that any such museum visits in the future would be made on my own. Thousands of museum visitors accompanied me as we all considered how far we have come, how much we have been blessed, and why this nation matters. Nothing sums up that belief more than a view of the "Star-Spangled Banner," tattered by battle, remembered in our national anthem, and a worthy predecessor to those flags carried in times of both peace and war. My question reappeared as the sun slipped slowly behind the Washington Monument and as I traveled once again by the White House in search of a warm place for dinner, eventually found on 16th Street, where a kindly waitress poured copious amounts of coffee for a chilled and weary traveler.

Warm, full, and again in need of rest, a return to my hotel room preceded a call home to check on everyone and a quick look at my e-mail. A week before, I had struggled with a medical concern followed by a biopsy. Day after day, I awaited results. Did I have cancer? Would my life be shortened or affected by treatments? Could I afford any of those with three children in college? Did my life matter very much anyway? What had I accomplished? Would anybody miss me if I were gone? Had I served God to the best of my ability, or was I more worried about accumulating "things"? A good biopsy report brought immediate relief, but the experience had changed me. I was more thankful and cognizant that our time here matters. Determined to pray more, to be thankful more, and to matter more, I ended my day on my knees, alone in a hotel room, emotional and in awe of my heavenly Father and his tender mercies. I have questioned God before, and he has answered, encouraged, corrected, and helped me many, many times. But at the end of the prayer, I had one question of myself, a question no doubt affected by my health crisis and the same one posed in my journeys around Washington, DC. The question is simple: *Is there an end?*

CHAPTER 2

Really?

I wish I had an answer to that because I'm
tired of answering that question.
—Yogi Berra

I am not a cold-weather fan; give me ninety-plus-degree days anytime. When enduring cold weather, I long for spring and fishing trips. Not that I go fishing that much now, but fishing is inextricably linked to pleasant days at local ponds or Lake Lanier, near my North Georgia home. During my childhood, springtime Saturdays began with morning visits to the local bait shop, where my dad or grandfather would swap stories and buy worms and minnows. Ritz crackers, sardines, and deviled ham were purchased to avoid hunger during a long day of fishing. Sun-dappled dirt roads led to favorite fishing spots, and occasionally we launched Dad's tiny boat to fish in coves where bass, crappie, and bream were vigorously pursued. A glimpse of a greenish, cold pond on a bright December day reminded me of clanky tackle boxes, Zebco 33s, and tangled fishing lines, which my grandfather would, with great patience, untangle. Keeping up with three grandsons around hooks and water probably stressed Grandfather and Grandmother greatly, but I don't ever recall a complaint. Well, there was that one time when my brother hooked me in the earlobe while casting with all of his might. Happy not to have been slung into Lake Lanier, I realized that a barbed hook has a purpose, and that purpose is to hold onto a biting fish with great tenacity. Grandfather suffered from essential tremor, making his hands very shaky. But those less-than-stable hands were determined to remove the hook from my earlobe. Using rusty pliers for a better grip, Grandfather pulled and tugged on the recalcitrant hook without success while I developed a newfound empathy for hooked fish. I was indeed thankful for the decision to quit fishing and visit the local emergency room. Upon our arrival, the ER physician looked a bit puzzled at my ear, which sported not only a hook but also a worm, lead weights, and some fishing line. The physician offered a one-word expletive that I will leave to your vivid imagination. I will say that that one word pretty well summed up my ridiculous condition. An emergency room nurse laughed out loud at the sight of my fashionable earring. A snip of the fishing hook and a tetanus shot later, I was ready to fish again.

My stories about fishing are more about mishaps than the ones that got away, but I miss fishing with my dad and grandfather. My sons fill in when they are home from college. Old guys tend to find kindred fishing spirits who venture to distant fishing holes where swapping stories and eating Ritz crackers, sardines, and deviled ham assumes mythical status.

I don't want to wish time away as I urge warm weather's return and at least the possibility of fishing again. I've concluded that our wish for time to pass is always granted. At fourteen or fifteen, I couldn't wait to drive a car. As a law student, classes crept by. I wanted desperately to make a living and begin a family. At fifty-seven, I wonder where all the time went and why I didn't fish more in the warm days of youth. I don't have a good answer to that question.

Unanswerable questions are annoying. Businesses devise elaborate decision-making tools and matrices to help, but some questions are so complex, so tattered, and so mercurial that many are treated like the neighbor no one understands. Eventually those questions and neighbors are left alone, rejected and ignored. Ignorance is indeed bliss, unless you ask, *"Is there an end?"*

The answer is as simple as the question. Yes, there is an end. Sorry, I thought you realized that. Otherwise, I would have sugarcoated it or left you guessing at least a little while longer. Sometime in the fifth grade, a time when I was rapidly maturing and absorbing much of the world around me, I bolted upright in my bed one night as I realized for the first time in my then young life that I would someday die. This realization occurred during the Cold War, a time when I understood that the former Soviet Union had nuclear weapons pointed at Atlanta, Georgia, and nearby Air Force bases. I realized that thermonuclear war meant fallout, radiation, massive fireballs, destruction, and, yes, death. Occasionally someone in the community would die from old age or an accident, and visits to the local funeral home—which smelled of an odd concoction of perfume, formaldehyde, and flowers—were inevitable. Those visitations were and are a poignant reminder that there is an end. Those reminders are also in our history books. Nations and kingdoms rise and fall with predictable regularity. Businesses prosper for a season and then fail due to the economy or competitive pressures. Some adapt and succeed; some never see the need to change. The same is true for governments, churches, and people. Our lives are a fabric of ups and downs. Some never get over the downs, some never get over the ups, and some can't tell the difference.

In late November 1963, on the eve of a long Thanksgiving weekend, word rushed through my elementary school that President Kennedy had been shot. We later learned of his death. That long weekend of constant television coverage, grieving, and reflection affected many, including me. President Kennedy's children had lost a father, something I took very seriously. I loved my dad and could not imagine losing him. Our nation had lost a leader, a leader who had guided us through the very real Cuban Missile Crisis. I would soon learn that President Kennedy loved the third chapter of Ecclesiastes, and that would become my Scripture of choice if I was selected to read in church or Sunday school. Ecclesiastes 3:1–11 so eloquently states the following:

1   To every thing there is a season, and a time for every purpose under the heaven;

2   A time to be born, and a time to die; a time to plant, and a time to pluck up that which is planted;

3   A time to kill, and a time to heal; a time to break down, and a time to build up;

4   A time to weep, and a time to laugh; a time to mourn, and a time to dance;

5   A time to cast away stones, and a time to gather stones together; a time to embrace, and a time to refrain from embracing;

6   A time to get, and a time to lose; a time to keep, and a time to cast away;

7   A time to rend, and a time to sew; a time to keep silence, and a time to speak;

8   A time to love, and a time to hate; a time of war, and a time of peace.

9   What profit hath he that worketh in that wherein he laboureth?

10   I have seen the travail, which God hath given to the sons of men to be exercised in it.

11 He hath made every thing beautiful in his time: also he hath set the world in their heart, so that no man can find out the work that God maketh from the beginning to the end.

While we may not know what God will make or do from beginning to the end (note the word *end*), we do know that God has a plan for our lives and our nation. And while we may not know specifics, I believe we do know when God is moving and preparing us for the times that will follow. I did not say "end times," just a time of transition, a time of change, and a time for another purpose. I do not assume a role of prophet or predictor of God's will—God forbid I ever do that—but God is speaking to many, urging preparation and precaution, provoking a sense of urgency, calling us to study, and offering his protection.

My youthful days of fishing ended. My time to drive came soon enough. My law school career ended, followed by beginning a family and making a living. My time with Granddad ended too.

There will someday be an end to us, our families, our ways of life, fishing lakes, this nation, wealth or lack thereof, our jobs, Congress, the Supreme Court, the White House, the Constitution, the Bill of Rights, Smithsonian Museums, lobbyists along K Street, corruption, fear, and tears. There is an end to politics as usual, to evil, to death, to budget deficits, to so many wearing victimhood and entitlement as a badge of honor, to war, to funeral homes, to hospitals, to protestors, to pain, to strife, to nuclear weapons, and to hunger.

Only God and his Word are eternal. But for your soul, nothing you touch or own will last or endure. Absolutely nothing.

The words *annoying, skeptical, disturbing, treasonous, rebellious, untrue, angry, sacrilege, harsh, scary, encouraging, historical, predictable,* and *surprising* could all be used to sum up what you think of my assertion. You may just ask, "Really? Did I need to hear all of that?

I liked the fishing stories, especially the one with hook dangling out of your ear, but I don't want to hear about an end of things. I have a beautiful wife and smart kids who are doing great in school and soccer and baseball. My job pays well, and we have a new house and great cars. Life is good. Why do you have to remind me that it all ends? I know the kids will grow up, my wife and I will age, we'll retire someday and enjoy the beach like we have always wanted, and the children and grandchildren will join us during long summers and at holidays, and it will just be all as planned. There will be no cancer, job loss, heart attacks, divorces, death, separations, wars or anything that will stand in the way of my dream life. Will there?"

The realization that God is in charge and we are not is scary and, to some, very annoying. Type A personalities have an especially hard time accepting that anyone else is in control. (I speak from firsthand experience, having been long classified as a Type A.) Being annoyed and scared causes us to move, to react, to begin thinking, and to begin changing. Some of those changes must include intense evaluation. What does our ideal nation look like? What does my ideal life look like? What does my ideal relationship with my family look like? What does my ideal relationship with God look like? And those annoying questions lead us to another answer. Periodically, every institution and every life must experience some form of revolution, reformation, and redirection. And each of those experiences will lead to one of only three results: utter destruction, renewal, or more of the same.

When we think of something ending, we think only of destruction and loss. Are you able to rethink that normal, grieving, and very human response? If you are able to do so, think restoration; think rising from the ashes, starting all over again, and unbridled renewal. That is what God has in store for us, along with a fascinating journey and experience.

More of the same means missed opportunities and, eventually, utter destruction. Who wants that?

You may have more questions, though, like, Why is all "this" going on? What is "this," anyway? Where did "this" come from? What is to come of us? Why all the odd beliefs? Why the attacks on our institutions and ways of life? And then there's the ever-present question: *What happened?*

"What happened?" is capable of being answered too. The answer is simply that there are profound consequences to our decisions and choices, good or bad. I am not talking judgment, just good sense. If you stick your hand into a fire, you get burned. If you eat healthfully, you might feel better and be healthier. If you love and are loyal to those around you, they might reciprocate. If you attend church and teach your children right and wrong, they will have an increased chance of being healthy, functional, godly adults. If you love your spouse, life will be happier. This is not rocket science. God may have a destiny and a plan for us, but we can run those plans into a ditch, mailboxes, and barbed-wire fences before we figure out that the road was a better option. Spending too much, working too little, expecting someone else to "fix it," seeking only pleasure, and forgetting God and godly ways of life are decisions with consequences. There is no such thing as casual sex or recreational drug use. Both have dramatic, even deadly, consequences. Moms and dads really matter, and so do God's Word, our word, our obligations, our honor, and our beliefs. God matters above all, and denial of lifetime and eternal consequences in an increasingly pluralistic society is a deadly sin placed clearly at the feet of everyone, especially churches and religious leadership too afraid to teach Jesus Christ and preach right or wrong in fear that people will leave and take their checks with them. In eternity, no church, government, or program will step in to absolve and save us from our indiscretions. Whether you believe in

God or not, there is an eternity. In reality, no government or program has or ever will correct poor choices and decisions. Believing differently is a bad choice with bad consequences. We now see a 15 trillion dollar deficit for this country and looming economic and social issues, which few in leadership positions are capable of addressing or changing.

All that is what happened. And there is an end to it.

CHAPTER 3

Do You Hear the Rain?

And Elijah said to Ahab, Get thee up, eat and drink;
for there is a sound of abundance of rain.
—1 Kings 18:41

We all have heroes. Standing on the crest of Mount Carmel in Israel on a bright spring day in 2009, overwhelmed by the beauty of the fertile Jezreel Valley stretching eastward toward Mount Gilboa, I remembered one of my heroes. Very few times in life do we get to walk where one of our heroes walked; I was visually and spiritually overwhelmed. Looking west to view the Mediterranean Sea, I wondered how he knew. Did he hear the rain? Did God speak to him and no other? What did others think when he predicted rain when none had fallen for several years? Did they laugh at him? Did he know confrontation would place a price on his head? Did he realize he would soon be alone, exhausted, and ready to give up?

There are many reasons for my admiration of Elijah, some very personal, some complex, and some very simple. He didn't mind a good fight; he was bold and very human. Perhaps that is enough, but Elijah's relationship with God was unique, so spellbinding and so fascinating that I cannot help being in awe of this man who left this world 848 years before Christ's birth. Maybe I understand some hardships, dangers, and loneliness, and his example speaks to my heart.

Maybe the real reason Elijah is my hero is because I hear the rain coming too—abundant rain.

Playing outdoors as children, we would scurry into the house when we heard a summer shower approaching. Spattering leaves in the forest, rain did not sneak up on us very often. But coming abundant rain is different, overdue, and a great surprise to many.

Growing up in rural North Georgia, we hungered for something exciting. Sure, there were baseball and basketball games, but occasionally something would shake up our small community. Car thieves, inebriated circus workers, and the occasional heretic were all of interest, but the frequency of exciting events left much to be desired. During those "dry spells," kids would tie ropes to hubcaps or scarecrows along roadways and, when someone stopped, hubcaps and scarecrows would surprisingly launch into the bushes followed by laughter and escape. Or perhaps we would dam up creeks just to later breech the dam for all manner of torrent and destruction downstream. (This mischief probably explains why I did not fish more in my youth.) While those events broke some of the monotony of growing up, there was always one exciting event we could count on—thunderstorms.

Thunderstorms sent old-timers to "storm pits," hollowed-out places in road banks where snakes and spiders resided. In a storm, all were tolerated. Tales of storms blowing down churches or moving houses from foundations were common. Before Doppler radar, almost every storm was a threat. I found those storms fascinating and actually looked forward to the eerie calm that would precede really bad storms. Retreating into our homes to play games, listen for thunder, and watch strobe-like lightning, fond memories were formed. Our surrender to one of nature's great exhibitions was rewarded with a moment of family togetherness.

Fueled by fond memories, my fascination with storms increased as I became older. I became quite a weather watcher. When my daughter was a child, she was particularly frightened by storms. Often I would hold her and watch the distant fireworks of a late evening storm, talking gently about the power of those bolts and God, the creator of all. She is now a beautiful young lady, and we still enjoy watching storms together, so much so that we have resolved to try our hand at storm chasing.

Rain awakens a dry earth with life-giving water. Rain washes down the filth we accumulate along our journey. Dust settles, lakes and streams are replenished; the world is refreshed.

I often wonder if we are living in the eerie stillness before a great storm. Is any coming storm welcomed? Will that storm bring us together? Will we surrender to one of God's great exhibitions? Will any coming storm change our politics, our families, the economy, and most everything we have come to expect? Is the "storm pit" simply a place to hide from God? Are you ready to embrace the excitement and refreshment of the coming storm? Will the storm pass us by? Should it? How severe will that storm be? Will there be destruction?

Nearing the completion of this writing, I traveled to my favorite prayer place. Only a few minutes from home, Burnt Mountain near Jasper, Georgia, offers a vista from the Appalachian foothills to Atlanta and beyond. On a very clear day, one might see tiny vehicles traveling on Atlanta expressways or have a clear view of a dramatic mountain known as Sharp Top. On a chilled September morning, just as the sun rose, fog blanketed hills below. The shadow of Burnt Mountain stood in contrast to the bright sun beaming on flatlands stretching south to the sea. I could see forever! The sight was breathtaking, but so was praying to my heavenly Father on a beautiful morning.

On my early morning drive to Burnt Mountain, I noted something unusual. Trees were down, roof damage was very much evident, and some older houses were essentially destroyed. Tornadoes generated by Tropical Storm Lee had left a trail of destruction. Debris littered the roadway, but life had quickly resumed: businesses were open and school buses and cars were en route to destinations. To my knowledge, no one died or was injured in that storm. Construction workers and roofers gained plenty of work for a few days, as did cleanup crews. In the middle of a recession, that storm brought good news to some. Many homeowners would receive new shingles and some home repair courtesy of Lee. Accounts of "freight train" noises and outdoor furniture flying through the air dominated cell phone calls and the evening news for a few days. Stories of the storm will be told for many, many years to come because, while there was damage, there was also thankfulness to be alive accompanied by many answered prayers offered in the midst of a storm. Lee's influence on a small North Georgia community provided great insight. Even though storms can be dangerous and create fear, the aftermath is not always bad. Excitement, prayers, restoration, refreshment, renewal, and thankfulness were all results of a dangerous storm.

My hero, Elijah, experienced a great storm in his life. In 1 Kings 19:1–5, we read the following:

1   And Ahab told Jezebel all that Elijah had done, and withal how he had slain all the prophets with the sword.

2   Then Jezebel sent a messenger unto Elijah, saying, So let the gods do to me, and more also, if I make not thy life as the life of one of them by to morrow about this time.

3   And when he saw that, he arose, and went for his life, and came to Beersheba, which belongeth to Judah, and left his servant there.

4   But he himself went a day's journey into the wilderness, and came and sat down under a juniper tree: and he requested for himself that he might die; and said, It is enough; now, O LORD, take away my life; for I am not better than my fathers.

5   And as he lay and slept under a juniper tree, behold, then an angel touched him, and said unto him, Arise and eat.

Elijah's time on earth was marked by great darkness. Those in power, Queen Jezebel and King Ahab, despised God and Elijah, too. During those evil rulers' reign, droughts, hunger, war, persecution, and an incredibly immoral religion dominated life in Israel. Despite God's victories and provision for Elijah, the old prophet became so weary that he gave up on life. Jezebel was still queen, and she clearly wanted Elijah dead. Elijah's earlier challenge to those in power and to licentious lifestyles resulted not in reform but in Elijah's becoming a fear-filled fugitive, stressed beyond imagination and likely unsure of his faith in God. Those who have challenged modern-day Jezebels intimately understand Elijah's unsettling journey. When our Christian beliefs are challenged, fear can rapidly replace faith, and boldness becomes just another word. With a bounty on his head, Elijah ran and ran far. Likely hundreds of Jezebel's followers, all wishing to please their pagan queen, fanned out in search of Elijah and their chance at infamy. God's hand on Elijah meant nothing to those in search of accolades, wealth, and power. Taking a man's life was secondary to those in search of a better life. Compassion and principle exited; opportunity and "self" mattered above all. I can almost hear one of the queen's followers say, "It's just business."

Elijah soon melted into a puddle of self-pity, gave up, and asked God to take his life. You are probably surprised that I would admire a quitter, but that moment of weariness, of despair, of forlornness is perhaps when

I admire Elijah most. In that moment, Elijah reveals himself to be very human, flawed, and just like me. As a husband, dad, and lawyer, I desperately desire to be strong and unshakable. When life beats me up, I become weak, weary, down and out, and no doubt, just like Elijah. I don't like admitting weakness. I should be better, stronger in my faith, firmer in my character and my resolve, but when I am tossed in a violent storm that never lets up, when nothing I have stood for and believe in seems to matter, when my life seems so worthless and without lasting benefit, why keep fighting? Are those struggles uniquely my own, or do I have plenty of company? You will have to answer that annoying question, but I expect many kindred spirits to nod their heads, fully understanding why Elijah speaks to me.

When we give up on ourselves, we give up on most everything and everyone around us too. I've heard it before: Politicians and corruption have ruined the country. Churches don't help anyone; they just judge and run people off. Nobody wants to work anymore. Marriage means little in a day of modern families. Drugs and alcohol have taken over. Many have become an unmotivated mess of jealously and entitlement, waiting for a lottery win or a lawsuit to find Easy Street. Life just leaves us dumbfounded and stuck under the "juniper tree," where motivation, hope, and faith become distant, almost unrecognizable, and eventually unimportant.

Slumbering too long in those conditions is very dangerous. Jezebel's followers catch up. Enemies know when there is no fight left in us, and those same enemies constantly search for our weaknesses. Elijah was in spiritual and physical danger while slumbering. Have we slept so long that our families and nation are now exposed to all manner of spiritual and physical danger? Have we evolved into beliefs that blessings are deserved, that we are somehow a chosen people solely because of our location and heritage? Do we believe our lifestyles and beliefs are impeccable and unassailable and that God will conveniently show up when we decide he is needed?

Regardless of conditions and attitudes, our loving heavenly Father understands battered and needy souls. Remarkably, he loves us when we don't even love ourselves. God's plan for our lives includes times of correction, humility, loneliness, despair, reflection, self-pity, repentance, restoration, inspiration, motivation, and questioning everything. When everything about us has been destroyed by storms, bad decisions, and those who would harm us; when nothing else matters; when we have tried our best and seemingly failed; when nothing ever goes right; when we are bare, raw, and vulnerable, our heavenly Father takes over and loves us, dusts us off, binds our wounds, and feeds us, too! Understand that God is so ready to do all this for our families and our nation, despite ourselves. And that is not all, by any means. The passage in 1 Kings 19:8–19 tells the rest of the story.

8   And he arose, and did eat and drink, and went in the strength of that meat forty days and forty nights unto Horeb the mount of God.

9   And he came thither unto a cave, and lodged there; and, behold, the word of the LORD came to him, and he said unto him, What doest thou here, Elijah?

10 And he said, I have been very jealous for the LORD God of hosts: for the children of Israel have forsaken thy covenant, thrown down thine altars, and slain thy prophets with the sword; and I, even I only, am left, and they seek my life, to take it away.

11 And he said, Go forth, and stand upon the mount before the LORD. And, behold, the LORD passed by, and a great and strong wind rent the mountains, and brake in pieces the rocks before the LORD; but the LORD was not in the wind: and

after the wind an earthquake; but the LORD was not in the earthquake:

12 And after the earthquake a fire; but the LORD was not in the fire: and after the fire a still small voice.

13 And it was so, when Elijah heard it, that he wrapped his face in his mantle, and went out, and stood in the entering in of the cave. And, behold, there came a voice unto him, and said, What doest thou here, Elijah?

14 And he said, I have been very jealous for the LORD God of hosts: because the children of Israel have forsaken thy covenant, thrown down thine altars, and slain thy prophets with the sword; and I, even I only, am left, and they seek my life, to take it away.

15 And the LORD said until him, Go, return on thy way to the wilderness of Damascus: and when thou comest, anoint Hazael to be king over Syria:

16 And Jehu the son of Nimshi shalt thou anoint to be king over Israel: and Elisha the son of Shaphat of Abelmeholah shalt thou anoint to be prophet in thy room.

17 And it shall come to pass, that him that escapeth the sword of Hazael shall Jehu slay; and him that escapeth from the sword of Jehu shall Elisha slay.

18 Yet I have left me seven thousand in Israel, all the knees which have not bowed unto Baal, and every mouth which hath not kissed him.

19 So he departed thence, and found Elisha the son of Shaphat, who was plowing with twelve yoke of oxen before him, and he with the twelfth: and Elijah passed by him, and cast his mantle upon him.

For forty days, Elijah traveled a distance of two hundred miles on foot, alone, without food, to Mount Horeb. Known as the delivery site of the Ten Commandments, Mount Horeb is often referred to as the Mountain of God. I wondered if Elijah was spiritually drawn to Mount Horeb or if he was searching for God. Perhaps Elijah wanted to complain in person. Never far away, God questioned Elijah. "Why are you here?" God is asking the same question to all of us. Why the cave? Why the long journey? Why the despair? Why the pity party? Elijah vented in his response. Paraphrasing 1 Kings 19:14 it is easy to sense Elijah's frustration through the ages: "I have fought for you, Lord, Israel has fallen away, destroyed your altars and your prophets and now I am under a death sentence. No one is left but me and look at where I am."

Recently I watched a television documentary depicting a horrible Vietnam era battle known as Hamburger Hill. Many American lives were lost taking that hill, and at the end of the battle, someone posted a sign upon the crest of that bloody ridge posing a simple question: "Was it worth it?" Elijah asked God this same question. God could have responded in anger, and he had every right to do so. Yet God's loving response was patient and demonstrative. God simply asked Elijah to watch. As God passed by, a great windstorm broke rocks and wreaked havoc on the mountain. God was not in the destruction and neither was he in the earthquake or fire that followed. I have often imagined Elijah standing in the mouth of that cave before a broad view. Likely frightened by violent events not fully understood by ancient man, Elijah was unresponsive until God's still small voice spoke. Only then did Elijah cover his face with that famous mantle. While he may have complained one more time, I sense that the weariness exited Elijah, inspiration returned, and hope reluctantly filled a void gouged out by fear in the old prophet. In the midst of storms and destruction around us, will not that same still, small voice say, "Peace, be still"?

God's voice made Elijah matter again. If we listen, America matters again, our families matter again, and so does our role in this world. After storms, after destruction, after fear, after everything else, a still, small voice challenges us to reenter significance, to get back to work, to change a world in need of God and a savior. Our complaints and fears captured in the cave of our self-pity and resignation mean nothing when God calls and we respond. And God has been calling, begging, pleading for his children to return. When we ignore those calls, storms become God's method of garnering our attention. Elijah's cave becomes a storm pit. Think about our economy, our stressed governments, wars, and so many conditions that prove us to be inadequate, ill-equipped, and downright incompetent. Sitting in a storm pit or in the house while the storm passes by is not an adequate response. Is it not time to come out and soak in a refreshed earth where fear wilts and boldness appears like the sun after the passing of a strong storm? *Is not the storm where Christians thrive, serve, and share a peace that the world does not understand?* If not now, when? If not us, then who?

Elijah was called to complete three tasks, and those tasks would lead to two new kings. One king would conquer Ahab's and Jezebel's kingdom; another would become their successor on the throne. Elijah's successor, Elisha, would also be called. A new generation of leaders was coming to power, old abuses and concepts were ending, and change, God's change, made an immediate, dramatic appearance in a desert cave. We shouldn't be too surprised because God's son would many years later make his entrance in a stable. Remarkably, historic visitors to Mount Horeb, Elijah and Moses would one day appear on another mountaintop with Jesus.

Elijah's tasks mattered; his story matters, but so does our own. Despite our storm-tossed existence, our journey to anoint another generation leads us back to God. To believe in restoration of this nation and Christian faith is not folly or unimaginable but part of our destiny. God corrected Elijah's misconception that he was alone. God had always been with Elijah, and thousands had braved the terrors of Ahab and Jezebel without ever worshiping a false god. You are not alone. However young or old, you matter a great deal.

Symbolically, Elijah represents Christianity and that representation includes a Christianity at a crossroads, very certain of promises and perseverance but uncertain as to relevance and effectiveness. In essence, Christianity under threat and persecution has retreated to a cave, wondering if anyone of similar belief even exists. Distraught and fearful, unaware that God has an imminent and important role for Christians in a modern world, Christianity awaits God's voice. Many are deafened by dramatic events and their search for God in all the wrong places. A few hear that same still, small voice. Those listening will soon anoint God's chosen successors.

Ahab and Jezebel represent our corrupt and destructive culture, and please make no mistake that culture includes governments, Hollywood, extremists, and, yes, religion, as many now define it. Those chosen by God and confirmed by Elijah represent a coming warrior generation ready to implement God's will. God prepared an enemy, a citizen, and a prophet to serve. Ahab and Jezebel survive today only as bywords for evil. After rain, change came to Israel.

Abundant rain is coming. Listen. Raindrops are already spattering a long-dry land, hungry for change, refreshment, and God. Coming rain is simply unprecedented restoration and renewal of the United States of America.

CHAPTER 4

Are You Ready for Some Big Events?

If you do not change direction, you may
end up where you are going.
—Lao Tzu

While sharing this writing with my college-age son, he posed a very relevant question: "Who are you to make predictions and observations? You are not a prophet. You are Dad. I know you and know how you think and observe, but who else knows you?" Fair enough. My son provided a needed reality check with a healthy dose of humility. What sane person in this whole wide world believes that the United States and its people are nearing renaissance? Am I alone? Are my questions simply a device to wish and hope for the good old days of prosperity and respect for a nation now mired in war, divisions, and economic chaos?

On a warmer winter's day, I visited a local park. There I was surprised to find dozens of people playing soccer and lacrosse. Most surprising were some dads and sons throwing baseballs and taking batting practice. With much of winter remaining and at least a couple of months before most everyone would even think about baseball, here were devoted players, practicing and preparing for an upcoming season. I realized that spring would come soon enough, as would baseball season. I also realized that those baseball players were an early sign of predictable events, as were the first jonquils emerging from cold winter soil.

A portion of my commute takes place through a pine forest where many trees have succumbed to a pine beetle infestation. On a windy day, a few of those trees, known by hunters as widow makers, will inevitably fall. Some fall onto the roadway, while others fall harmlessly in the forest. One tree leaned so precariously over the roadway that I eventually prohibited my family from traveling this route. Each morning's commute revealed the tree leaning more closely to a fall. I was thankful for each unscathed passing. Eventually, county road maintenance crews removed the threat, but predicting that the tree was due for a fall was not prophecy—just common sense.

When one surveys the condition of our country and our people, common sense observations lead to many predictions. Those predictions are not some mystical or spooky prophecies but the result of legitimate concerns about our families and our country. Observant citizens might ask, Are we a unique nation? Are we truly free or regulated to death? Do our citizens value liberty or security? *Are we really exceptional or just riding along on past successes? Could we as a nation be better, do better, be freer?* Is it possible for our land to become less legalistic, more caring, more industrious, and more competitive? Are we capable of becoming more faithful, less divided, more loving, and more concerned about others? These questions are not unique to our time. History records the occasional appearance of those who "march to a different drummer" posing annoying, compelling questions that challenge everything. Those daring to question are often hated, ridiculed, and placed in great danger. Daring questions often emanate from fascinating lives and will on occasion lead to big events. I am a dad and not at all that fascinating, daring, or threatened. I do claim to be a good observer and to love history. I also claim to be desperately in love with my family and my Lord. Those two loves, those passions, cause me not only to ask questions but compel remembrance of predecessors who risked their lives and reputations simply by asking questions.

Five hundred years ago, annoying questions were flooding Europe. New World discoveries were beginning in earnest as young men and women dreamed of foreign shores, riches, opportunities, and adventure. Despite dangers and the very real risk of death and failure, young people asked, "Why not now?" and "Why not me?" A willingness to embrace renaissance concepts of freedom and human dignity led to an exodus from rampant political, religious, and social oppression. One of the most remarkable "big events" in history began with questions, discontent, and a healthy dose of wanderlust. The exploration and settlement of the New World would later be marred by slavery and the foul treatment of indigenous peoples, but that "big event" nevertheless changed the world.

I would not be writing this book if those events hadn't happened. I would likely not exist. If my parents had even existed, they likely would have never met or, at best, I would have grown up in my ancestral County Suffolk of England, fully aware of an impenetrable caste system. I would have experienced a domineering church and, if discontent, persecution for being a Baptist, all the while living in a poorer, declining, and likely divided country. Even worse, without those big events, Germany could have won either of the world wars occurring during the twentieth century, and the former U.S.S.R. might have dominated most of the world by this time. Our discovery and existence as a nation did matter, and it matters a great deal going forward. We are products of a big event.

With regularity, good men and women living in the right era are necessary to serve as an abundant rain, to lead, to bring a storm of thought and challenge. Their presence and actions alter political and social landscapes. Consider a few examples from previous eras.

Almost two thousand years ago, men and women willingly gave their lives for a cause, a cause embodied in one man—Jesus Christ. His perfect life was sacrificed so that men and women could experience a personal relationship with God. That cause made little sense to leaders paralyzed in tradition, but many men and women followed regardless of assured persecution. Eventually, the mightiest nation on earth at the time would adopt Christianity. Nothing would ever be the same again.

When the Catholic Church became corrupt and alienated many of its members, the time was right for challenge and change. As a twenty-seven-year-old man, Martin Luther observed those flawed conditions and theology that would lead him in 1517 to issue his courageous 95 Theses. Others with similar ideas had been burned as heretics, and no doubt a similar fate awaited Luther. Yet some causes are so important and so vital that fear and retaliation mean nothing. Martin Luther's stand inspired others to challenge corrupt authority that had existed for hundreds of years. Without Martin Luther's boldness, the American and French Revolutions might never have occurred. Newton and Locke may have well suppressed ideas that inspire and challenge even today. Luther's challenges changed the world.

During the late eighteenth century, twenty-eight-year-old William Wilberforce began a long battle to abolish slavery in England. Although ostracized by some, Wilberforce's tireless efforts eventually won over the opposition and inspired others in the United States—an inspiration that affected the abolitionist movement, politics, and divisions leading to the American Civil War. Those events eventually spawned the Civil Rights

Movement. Wilberforce's actions affected two continents and hundreds of thousands of men, women, and children who longed only to be free and able to determine their own destinies. Lives were lost and blood shed for a cause, a belief, a concept. We are products of that bloodshed and Wilberforce's radical belief in human dignity and freedom. He, too, changed the world.

A contemporary of Wilberforce's living on the other side of the Atlantic and the contemporaneous Revolutionary War, Thomas Jefferson believed that man's dignity and liberty were so important, so inalienable, that sacrifice of one's fortune, honor, and life were justified in preservation of those radical aspects of humanity. On the shoulders of a concept and a document, Jefferson's generation committed to a cause that led to the formation of the United States of America. That founding changed the world, saved lives, and shared the gospel of liberty with a world that continues its struggle with the radical concept of freedom.

In 1976, thirty-three-year-old Lech Wałęsa initiated a bold labor movement in communist Poland. Challenging the Soviet Union often led to confinement in a Siberian gulag, or worse, but Wałęsa's movement captured the world's imagination. Wałęsa's actions in support of student protests and workers adversely affected by rising food prices eventually led to his arrest, firing, and, finally, recognition for his charismatic stand for human rights in the Gdańsk shipyards. Wałęsa would later receive the Nobel Peace Prize and become president of Poland. His courage assuredly influenced the subsequent fall of the Berlin Wall and the eventual freedom of millions. Wałęsa was a world and game changer.

Martin Luther King Jr. boldly stood against racism when that stand offered significant risk and consequences in a nation simultaneously living in the aftermath of the Civil War and the dawning of the Space Age. An orator and organizer, King advocated societal change leading to equality for all races. Also a Nobel Peace Prize winner, Martin Luther

King Jr. paid for his destiny and vision with his life. The United States would never be the same and, for that matter, neither would the world. Freedom's clarion call—delayed, diffused, and difficult—would not be easily suppressed here or in nations across the planet. One man made a difference.

It is fair to ask if anyone among us now will change the world. Do we have any modern-day equivalents to Luther, Wilberforce, Jefferson, Wałęsa, and King? The answer is an emphatic yes. Young leaders prepared for this time in history are being readied right now. Understanding those leaders and their mission is vital to our families and our institutions. Nothing is going to be the same.

In an article posted online by the Pew Research Center, dated December 11, 2009, and entitled "The Millennials" by Scott Keeter and Paul Taylor (http://pewresearch.org/pubs/1437/millenials-profile; used with express permission) observations about a cohort of young people sharing an era and experiences were noted as follows:

- Millennials were born between 1980 and 2000.
- They are the most ethnically and racially diverse cohort of youth in the nation's history. Among those ages thirteen to twenty-nine, 18.5% are Hispanic; 14.2% are African-American; 4.3% are Asian; 3.2% are mixed race or other; and 59.8%, a record low, are Caucasian.
- They are starting out as the most politically progressive age group in modern history. In the 2008 election, Millennials voted for Barack Obama over John McCain by 66% to 32%, while adults aged thirty and over split their votes 50% to 49%. In the four decades since the development of Election Day exit polling, this is the largest gap ever seen in a presidential election between the votes of those under and over age thirty.

- They are the first generation in human history to regard behaviors like tweeting and texting, along with websites like Facebook, YouTube, Google, and Wikipedia, not as astonishing innovations of the digital era but as everyday parts of their social lives and their search for understanding.
- They are the least religiously observant youths since survey research began charting religious behavior.
- They are more inclined toward trust in institutions than were either of their two predecessor generations—Generation Xers (who are now ages thirty to forty-five) and baby boomers (now ages forty-six to sixty-four)—when they were coming of age.

The article also noted the following influences on all generations:

One is the *life cycle effect*. The biological impact of aging and the changing roles that people play as they grow older typically produce changes in attitudes and social behaviors over time. In short, young people may be different from older people today, but they may well become more like them tomorrow, once they themselves age.

The second is the *cohort effect*. Generation differences can be the byproduct of the unique historical circumstances that members of an age cohort experience during adolescence and young adulthood, when awareness of the wider world deepens and personal identities and values systems are being strongly shaped. The unique nature of the times imprints itself on each successive age cohort, producing differences that persist even as a cohort ages and moves through the life cycle.

In addition to life cycle and cohort effects, there are also *period effects*. These are major events (wars, social movements, scientific or technological breakthroughs) that are likely to have a simultaneous impact on all age groups, though, again, their impact is often greatest among the young because their values and habits are less fixed than those of other age groups.

Those analytical tools provide unique insight into multiple influences affecting Millennials. Many Millennials are strongly influenced, good or bad, by parents and grandparents. If that influence is positive, the life cycle effect of those parents' and grandparents' experiences, wisdom, and maturity programs the next generation far earlier than might be expected. In simple terms, certain Millennials are mature beyond their years because older members of their family or community cared enough to prepare them for what is to come based on what has been. Older belief structures are at least offered for consideration. Concerned about the future, parents and grandparents have defensively accelerated their influence over young lives. Some future leaders have actually listened, too.

Conversely, one must consider the potential for negative influence by parents and grandparents, assuming those elders are even around. Negative influence can lead to positive results, though. Rejection of destructive and divisive lifestyles by Millennials should be expected, a condition more fully discussed in Chapter 5.

Cohort effects are more complicated. Decades of attending school, playing sports and socializing with cohorts undoubtedly influences young leaders. Emerging leadership will quite often be caught between family and friends, a condition simultaneously creating tension and relationships. Emerging leaders actually care what their friends, parents, and grandparents think. Coping with often disparate belief structures creates very unique and adaptive responses while preparing young leaders for their future roles.

Period effects such as war, recession, national debt, and political divisions have at least partially defined emerging leaders. Unlike other generations, Millennials view technological advances not as threatening but as complementary, expected, and necessary. Many young adults do not recall a time of peace. Many are patriotic, supportive of the military, and driven to serve. Despite predictions to the contrary, certain Millennials will have little problem challenging institutions. Occupy Wall Street members are predominately Millennials and provide evidence of this capability, although I remain skeptical about politically active groups manipulating vulnerable and unemployed young people. Is it possible for a broad spectrum of Millennials to become disheartened about the government as a result of failed economic and social policies? Will Millennials evolve into distrusting institutions while adopting increasingly conservative political beliefs? One major factor must be considered: mediocrity and lowered expectations are not acceptable to a generation unaccustomed to second-rate living standards.

Questions abound. How does a group of young people who theoretically trust institutions more than prior generations did or do evolve into a force large enough to aggressively challenge the excesses of those same institutions? *How will one of the most diverse generations in the history of the nation coalesce into conservatism, reform, and renewal?* How will one of the most secular generations ever turn to God? How will our nation respond? Will you embrace their cause? Will you hate or hurt these young people when they challenge most everyone's comfort and power? Will your children or grandchildren be among these emerging leaders? What if that leadership exposes your child to harsh criticism and even death? Is any cause worth that price? Are some events just too big?

CHAPTER 5

Who Lives in That House?

Change your thoughts and you change your world.
—Norman Vincent Peale

My wife and I traveled to Virginia a few years back, where I visited many Civil War and Revolutionary War battlefields. She is a saint to endure my very detailed and hands-on visits to obscure battlefields, where I trace troop movements and consider the bravery of old combatants. Driving south of Charlottesville, Virginia, along bucolic byways, I noticed little houses dotting hillsides. One Virginia home sported an old-fashioned clothesline filled with colorful laundry fluttering on a gentle spring breeze. I wondered who lived there. Was this the home of a World War II veteran living out life in relative peace or a young family in a starter home, saving money using the sun and wind as a clothes dryer? Were children being reared there? What were they being taught? Did anyone go to church? Were any children influenced by grandparents? Were grandparents rearing their own grandchildren? Unfortunately, I had to consider abuse, hurt, and abandonment, too. Welcome to my vivid imagination. I'll likely never know what happens in those homes or the millions like them all over this nation. I can say that children occupying any of those houses are being trained and influenced in one manner or another in preparation for adulthood. That training and influence may be based in Christian principles or pop culture, secular humanism or humanitarianism.

Since first noticing those little houses, my thoughts about inhabitants have evolved radically. Earlier writings revealed a strong bias and belief that families with very traditional values would generate children destined to change our nation for the better. That belief was based in specious logic that good homes produce motivated children with good motives and values. We all realize that good homes and good parents do, on occasion, rear disastrous children. While I expect strong influence from children reared in good homes, other young people from different and less idealistic upbringings will and must participate in an unexpected and imminent national restorative movement. In fact, those with nontraditional backgrounds may be more disciplined and driven to offer superior leadership. (Do not assume that past influences and beliefs are unimportant, a topic to be discussed more fully in Chapter 7).

My bias favoring traditionally reared children is understandable. My parents stayed together, attended church, supported the PTA, coached baseball, and baked cookies for bake sales. Their example provided a road map for rearing my children despite my strong belief that I could avoid some of their mistakes. I did not. In fact, I repeated mistakes such as discussing in excruciating detail every one of my children's mishaps and errors on baseball fields or basketball courts during miserable postgame drives home. My parents imprinted parenting skills (or a lack thereof) so deeply that even mistakes were replicated. Good and bad traits are often copied by each successive generation with predictable mutations in circumstances, values, and personalities. A massive mutation occurred in the 1960s and 1970s when many Americans rejected war, patriotism, and convention and substituted personal exploration, experimentation, and, on occasion, even anarchy in a convulsion of countercultural excess. Those events led to a host of societal problems, including unprecedented drug usage, teen pregnancy, runaways, homelessness, and incredible damage to the institution of marriage. A definition of *countercultural* is mercurial, but during the 1960s that definition included significant numbers of antiwar and antigovernment advocates who oddly and eventually morphed into predominately liberal, antibusiness, and generally big-government supporting middle-agers. The countercultural movement eventually became more acceptable and more mainstream, as noted in the 2008 election of Barack Obama, himself the child of a countercultural mother.

Some baby boomers had little interest in pursuing lifestyles of the counterculturalists. In my community there are a number of cedar sided homes which were built in the 1970s and 1980s. During an era of high gasoline prices, shortages, inflation, Watergate, the Iran Hostage Crisis, recession and divisions over the Vietnam War, baby boomers built modern versions of the log cabin. At the same time, boomers started families. Simultaneously, television shows like *The Waltons* and *Little House on the Prairie* became very popular. During that era, homes, furnishings and pop culture revealed a widespread hunger for simpler times. Back to nature, back to basics, back to family values evolved into a significant influence on young families. Stop by any current yard sale and you will note quaint country themed items being sold which at first seem dated and irrelevant to our modern era. Those items are immensely relevant though. Similar to cedar sided houses, those relics symbolize rejection of conditions and values of the 1960s and 1970s. (Placement of those items in yard sales may have other implications including aging owners, different tastes and abandonment of earlier influences.)

Understand that possessions and the type of house one lives in do not define a life or a cause. Periodically someone in some house will hunger for understanding when conditions, events and eras are less than understandable. That hunger will often lead to a retreat to what is perceived as right and wholesome. That retreat will lead to some type of values and beliefs being emphatically taught to the next generation. Parents undertake that role naturally. Institutions, like government, are incredibly incapable of reflection, self-evaluation and correction. Churches struggle with similar limitations but many have recently retreated to foundational beliefs, especially those existent at the genesis of the New Testament. Individuals often retreat to traditions and ancestral values which can become irrelevant and paralytic but which also may lead to great insight and growth. For example, prior generations abhorred debt. Those beliefs are returning as contemporaries struggle with debt during a very deep recession.

Many Millennials have been forever influenced by their parents' rejection of what seemed to be an out of control America. Those baby boomer parents remembered and attempted to clone their own upbringings with notable exclusions, including a decline in church attendance and loss of confidence in government as a trustworthy institution. Many baby boomers handed down healthy doses of skepticism and extensive distrust of institutions to their own children.

I know this upbringing casts doubt as to whether Millennials will trust institutions, and while these children of Baby Boomers are influential, their numbers are small. Here is the fascinating part. Significant numbers of countercultural children have rejected the behaviors and lifestyles of their parents. Those children oddly find stability and commonality with contemporaries reared in traditional homes by parents who forty years ago rejected the same behaviors and the same counterculturalists. The convergence of two sets of young people with distinctly different upbringings, sharing skepticism and an insatiable desire to change the world, is complicated, incredible, and imminent. This convergence is the product of the rejection of countercultural beliefs and lifestyles by two generations who have simply had enough.

Countercultural beliefs have tested, tried, and pushed the limits of society for well over a generation. Rebellious counterculturalist children have grown weary of failure, addictions, and abuses that inevitably arose in past peak cultures. This concept eluded me because, to be honest, I had serious doubts that anything good came from countercultural homes and families. I was wrong.

The Georgia Legislature recently adopted a program granting college scholarships to high-performing middle-school children. While being interviewed, an eligible middle school student with great conviction commented that the scholarship was her "ticket out." Her choice of words was interesting. Something was wrong at home. As an early teen, she was ready to move on. She may have been subjected to poverty or abuse, or she may have been just incredibly ambitious. On the same day, one of my staff printed an article highlighting a homeless high school student who was excelling in a national science talent search.

And then there was Joel. He came to work for my law firm during his late teens as a "runner." For several years, he dependably carried documents to the courthouse, kept copiers full of paper, cleaned, copied, and did just about anything a dozen or so people asked. Joel lived precariously, one step away from homelessness, and yet he was one of the most contented, peaceful, and inspirational persons I have ever encountered. Joel's parents, for reasons never fully shared, moved away, leaving him and his sister to fend for themselves. I am not aware of any financial or emotional support ever offered by those parents. They left when Joel was attending college and his sister was finishing high school. Previously, Joel had been awarded top honors for his high school mathematics acumen, a feat soon replicated by his sister. Joel basically assumed the role of parent and tutor for his sister, a sister he loved very much, all the while working a second job preparing a chain restaurant for early morning breakfast service, attending college classes, working for my firm, buying a small house and a truck, and otherwise just thriving like no one I have ever witnessed. Joel also evidenced his profound love of God by eventually choosing studies preparing him for the ministry.

Joel did leave one other memory. Located in my office is a display cabinet where I keep precious belongings. Photographs, pottery from Israel, encouraging notes from clients, and models of tractors like my grandfather once owned are all showcased in that cabinet. An attractive inscribed wooden pen box is also located there, a Christmas present from Joel. Recently I read the very appropriate inscription again: "The righteous man walks in his integrity; his children are blessed after him" (Prov. 20:7 NKJV).

Joel's thoughtful gift spoke clearly. Righteousness and integrity lead to blessed children. Blessed children will help restore families and our nation. Children of good parents who challenge bad lifestyles and children of counterculturalists who do the same have been blessed with a vision and a heart that not everyone is privileged to experience. At some point, all societies face challenges to norms and mainstream beliefs. Our constant evolution and predilection for better will lead baby boomer parents, their children, and some children of the counterculture to stand against failure, immorality, and decline. At the core of these movements are young adults like Joel and motivated children of boomer parents, who are all exceptional and unexpected and who eventually fuse into a rare element of change.

Millennials are actively searching for worthy causes and heroes. A contrarian lifestyle and belief structure offered by traditionally and defensively reared children of boomers and rebellious children of the counterculture are enigmatic, attractive, and highly influential upon other Millennials. Instead of being rejected, those contrarian lifestyles will not only be tolerated by contemporaries but held in high esteem. That connection is underpinned by youth, shared experiences, and a perception that all are needed in an uncertain world. Expect bold stands as living standards deteriorate, opportunities decline, and government becomes increasingly dysfunctional. Adverse reaction will quickly occur, too. At some point, those in power and those benefited by those in power will persecute young people who stand for reform. (Remember King Saul pursuing David?) When persecution occurs, boomer parents will rush to the aid of their children. Security and safety will become secondary to protecting and supporting their offspring. Simultaneously, other less-reform-minded Millennials will join the fray in support of their brothers and sisters. (Social networking will play a huge role in connecting participants.) Recent revolutions in Egypt and other Middle Eastern countries showcase how young adults are capable of forcing rapid change upon corrupt and irrelevant governments.

The emergence of reformers joining parents and other Millennials to force change is entirely unexpected, dangerous, and, to be honest, a bit bizarre. Yet here is where the next American Revolution begins, with ideas and confrontation not unlike those at Concord, where anger, principle, and youth led to a moment heard around the world. Understanding a different group of contemporary young men and women willing to offer their lives for freedom and for others is, therefore, vital.

Ezekiel 22:30 states, "And I sought for a man among them, that should make up the hedge, and stand in the gap before me for the land, that I should not destroy it: but I found none." Young lives being launched from those little houses dotting the Virginia countryside or from the cedar sided home down the street matter a great deal. Without stable, moral, and motivated young people prepared for leadership and supported by parents and mentors, a great gap exists. That gap is the period between now and the future of this nation. The good news is that the hedge is being made up and the gap filled with precious lives from a variety of backgrounds just waiting for our heavenly Father to flip the switch and illuminate not only our failures but our destinies.

CHAPTER 6

Can We Stand the Heat?

Great hopes make great men.
—Thomas Fuller

In the late 1990s my family visited Yellowstone National Park. After coming through the south entrance, we were soon confronted with the remnants of a huge wildfire. Charred trees lined roadways for miles and miles and served as a reminder that devastation had once visited that beautiful place. To be honest, the view was disappointing—even depressing. Why did this wildfire happen in the crown jewel of our national parks? The answers were intriguing. In an effort to preserve the park and protect the public, the park's caretakers had suppressed fire for many years. Before man's intervention, fires naturally occurred, resulting in periodic removal of tinder and debris. Prohibiting fire actually allowed more fuel to accumulate. A seemingly logical act of suppressing fire increased the risk of devastating wildfire.

Fires stress trees and other vegetation; they turn beautiful forests into blackened, smoking, nasty places. But wait a while. Fire also removes competing plants, allowing more resilient trees and plants to become hardier. Fire removes the threat of wildfire, at least for a season. By analogy, consider that our national accumulation of policies, laws, methods, foul ideas, restraints, and beliefs must occasionally be obliterated. Obliteration opens new opportunities, enhances economies, and eventually clears heads and hearts. Like natural woodlands, lives and nations must regularly experience the removal of tinder and debris. These events mimic fire in that they come with danger, destruction, and disruption. Think the War between the States and our own American Revolution, and add in the World Wars for good measure. Millions of people died in those events, nations were devastated, monsters like Hitler and Stalin came into power, and mothers lost sons and daughters. Global politics and economies were changed, challenged, or invigorated by those dramatic events. It is fair to ask if we must live through similar events to restore our nation? Do events that are so cataclysmic and dangerous ever lead to anything productive? Is there some event less damaging yet equally cathartic? If that event is possible, what would it look like? Who would participate? Will the event resemble a brushfire or a wildfire? Must the whole forest burn?

Emerging young leaders discussed in the preceding chapter are carrying a torch poised to burn away tinder and debris we have allowed to accumulate in our lives and our nation for decades. With God's help, this will be a "controlled burn," one that removes dangerous fuel but does not destroy all else in the process. In doing so, the United States will experience unprecedented healing, prosperity, and resurgence. Scary events we all worry about need never happen; you won't need to stockpile ammunition or food to survive.

Many have written Millennials off as a generically self-absorbed, video-game playing, shallow, and virtually illiterate bundle of incompetents. Little do they realize that Millennials will have much in common with the World War II–era Greatest Generation. Because the emergence of godly leaders emanating from the Millennials is so unexpected, I reasoned that a new name for this group is appropriate. Why not call them the Unexpected Generation to note a subset of ← exceptional young people who are being prepared to lead our nation to restoration. This group already includes war veterans, missionaries, brilliant minds, college students, construction workers, teachers, pastors, and graduate degree-holders. Experienced but not yet jaded, these young people possess hope, optimism, and an inherent, insatiable desire to provide a life for their families that is as good as or better than what their parents have experienced. (As noted, some may resolutely reject their upbringings.) Many of these young people have struggled at one time or another. Instead of spewing complaints or blame, those difficulties tempered them and offered lessons about determination and overcoming adversity. Many have been affected by the scarcity of jobs and a poor economy. In lieu of protesting, many of these driven and called young people enlisted in the military or obtained advanced degrees. Most have worked tough, menial jobs or created their own employment. A large percentage of them understand hard work, hard times, and hard decisions—conditions that have prepared and readied them for their destiny.

Certainly not all Millennials have nation saving in their future. While the Occupy Movement talks much about the 99 percent, Unexpected Generation members are the true remaining 1%. The Occupy Movement has captured media attention, but Unexpected Generation members will capture the imagination and heart of our nation's hunger for renewal and leadership. These emerging leaders are unashamed of an agenda driven by personal responsibility and achievement. Their view is future driven, so past sins and wrongs committed by any group, however meritorious or instilled, are noted but secondary to reestablishing the preeminence of the United States. Lack of focus on the past will anger many. Unexpected Generation members will have no difficulty speaking truth and reality without regard for political or social implications. That contrast to our current political environment is shocking, edgy, and ultimately attractive. By the term *edgy*, I mean contrary to expected behaviors. *Edgy* may include political incorrectness, challenges to how we address race in this nation, repudiation of religious bureaucracy, confrontation with elected officials, and an outright assault on educational agendas developed over the past forty years. While the angry and threatened will not follow, many who are encouraged that reformation and renewal are at hand will gladly follow refreshing, candid, and youthful leadership. Even those who have given up on making a difference will gladly join a group with at least the potential to "shake things up."

Expect emerging young leaders to be very recognizable. In fact, start looking for them now. While I suspect many of those new leaders are Christian and conservative, I realize that will not entirely be the case. To reach broad segments of society, leaders must emerge from all faiths and races, glued together by their drive to restore a nation. All share a common goal, though: to provide the best possible environment for personal and economic liberty. These leaders will clearly understand competition and the importance of being exceptional as an individual and as a nation. Principles will once again be important. High performance will be expected in classrooms, athletic fields, and battlefields. A strong presence of suburban and rural participants will be noted, as will those coming from private schools and home schools, but do not rule out many young leaders emerging from public education, inner cities, and even the homeless. Bright young people have for some time resisted messages that permeate the public education curriculum, calling for conformity, compliance, and subtle retribution against capitalists and those rejecting race- and class-centric agendas.

While my children were attending public school, group projects ←
were frequently assigned. Often, less motivated students took advantage
of those willing to work and achieve. While educators sought to teach
teamwork, cooperation, and perhaps an insidious message about
collective efforts, the lesson actually taught was that not everyone
will perform at expected levels. Poorly performing students either
damaged the grade of the group or drove others to cover for their lack of
performance. Students accustomed to completing tasks and performing
well learned not to depend on others with little desire to perform. High-
performing parents likely shared similar workplace experiences. Lazy
and unmotivated students and workers eventually face the real world,
and the real world keeps score. Unexpected Generation members are
scorekeepers and competitors, and they are completely disinterested
in agendas that reward poor performance. Their example will have
a profound impact on other Millennials who eventually realize that
unearned grades and trophies do not continue beyond their teen years
and that we are people, not classes and races.

Unexpected Generation participants will throw many conventions
under the bus. Political parties will likely be considered nothing but
obstructionist and devoid of value, religious denominations (not God)
will become irrelevant, and the mantle of victimhood worn so proudly
by many individuals and groups will be considered evidence of weakness.
Quality education accompanied by unbridled, unconventional faith will
become not only very, very important but also very, very reformed as
we edge toward revolution.

Revolutions are dangerous business. Challenging, reconsidering,
and questioning most everything about ourselves, our society, our
institutions, and our government will prepare you for the mindset
of these young revolutionaries, but make no mistake: revolutions are
historically protracted, messy, and bloody. New leadership will seek

to avoid bloodshed, but one cannot entirely rule out the possibility. Because their goal is to reform a nation, we must have a nation at the end of the day. Founding fathers will once again become role models, and the Declaration of Independence and the Constitution will matter again. History will once again be significant and be taught without revision or political spin.

Unexpected Generation leaders will question profusely. Intense questioning of previously held beliefs makes us consider: Is this right? Why do I think that way? Where did that come from? Questioning on that level creates emotional and intellectual highs and lows that can be simultaneously frustrating and invigorating. Questioning on that level is also very threatening to victims of path dependency. Many current leaders perceive innovation and fresh ideas as threats rather than options. Unexpected Generation members will use skepticism, training in classrooms and business environments, and, for some, battlefield experiences to constantly evaluate options. While we hope and pray for good results, mistakes will be made. Revolutions are rare, and some on-the-job-training is absolutely necessary. Youthful leaders will definitely hunger for caring, supportive relationships with elders who understand the loneliness of leadership, especially when mistakes have been made.

While Unexpected Generation members will fascinate us, many around the world awaiting a spark of inspiration will be intrigued and motivated by this powerful group of young men and women. Recently I met someone whose family emigrated from Iran many years ago and who had not so long ago visited family in Tehran. Of course, I was curious about the country and its people. I was spellbound by stories about a country struggling with its role in the world. With over one million killed in the Iran-Iraq War followed by mass exodus, Iran is now occupied by a very large young adult population. Sensing little anti-Western sentiment, my acquaintance noted that change is coming to Iran in the not-so-distant future. Younger citizens of a country considered by many to be a pariah are anxious for greater freedom and better relationships with the rest of the world. Unless revolt similar to recent events in Egypt, Libya, and Syria occurs, my newfound friend believes that change is due sometime in the next decade.

Other observations included a sense that clerics and leaders like Ahmadinejad will have eroding influence and, essentially, no influence after the next generation assumes a rightful leadership role. Understanding how difficult that transfer of power will be and with a stoic, "it will happen" attitude, I was fascinated to hear a very correct perspective—that no condition lasts forever—emanating from a young man excited about what will eventually happen in his homeland. The only certainty in Iran or here in the United States is that change is inevitable.

Regardless of conditions or location, almost everyone on this planet possesses a dear hope for something better for themselves and those who follow. Oppressive governments and regimes always fall. Ways of life that dishonor human dignity and freedom are eventually obliterated by the wildfire of emotion and logic that builds and subsides in a symmetry and rhythm as old as man's existence.

Americans have experienced greater liberty and prosperity than Iranians will ever know. Waiting a decade might work in Iran, but not here. Liberty and the pursuit of happiness are not so patient. Neither are Unexpected Generation members, whose hearts and souls are on fire for our national and spiritual renewal.

CHAPTER 7

"Do Over," Anyone?

Nobody can go back and start a new beginning, but anyone can start today and make a new ending.
—Maria Robinson

Not long ago, operating software programmers created a handy tool known as "system restore." This tool is useful when computers fail to operate properly after installing a program or a virus attack. The concept behind system restore is simple: it returns the computer to a state in which it existed prior to the problem. In playground terms, that restoration is a "do over." We understand this concept when we comment, "I wish things were like they were before," or "I wish I could start over again." While Unexpected Generation members are very forward looking, they have developed a human version of "system restore" influenced by other lives and historical reference and concepts.

Reconstructing who influenced me the most helped with understanding my human "system restore." My paternal grandparents were first on the list. Their small home and even smaller bank account did not define their lives or influence. They endured the near loss of their only son, life in a mill town, farming in the middle of the Great

Depression, and a host of other challenges. Yet, the community was drawn to this couple, not because of wealth or beauty, but because they were encouraging, humorous, and strong. They never traveled more than five hundred miles from home, had limited education, possessed strong political and moral opinions, and didn't mind sharing those opinions with a friend or preacher. My grandparents certainly had their flaws, but they were leaders in their time and in their community. They were not afraid of difficult situations, such as when Grandfather was called upon to shoot rabid dogs menacing his community. (I did think of the mythical Atticus Finch doing the same thing in *To Kill a Mockingbird*.) My grandparents had no reservations about asking tough questions and confronting others when necessary, and in doing so, they were charismatic. Part of that charisma was that they genuinely cared for others and future generations. That care is why I remember those two, as do many others, decades after their passing. When I am uncertain, discouraged, or blessed, I think of those lives well lived and consider how they would handle my current situation, good or bad.

Others affected my life, too. The auto mechanic who spent time explaining the workings of an engine while sharing his unique philosophies with a curious college student comes to mind. His simple statement that "the sun doesn't shine like it used to" reminded me that our view of the world changes as we age. How do I forget my fourth-grade teacher who noticed my insatiable desire to read? Almost fifty years later, she fuels my passion with books she graciously delivers to my office. Also on that list is the minister who lived next door during my youth. His devotion to God, family, and lifelong learning offered a shining and long-remembered example. All of those people mattered. All share one common thread. Those so remembered were selfless and took time to care, to listen, to guide, and to love. Nothing about caring, listening, guiding, and loving is complex. The complexity comes with having enough time, sincerity, perspective, and knowledge to make a difference in another's life.

History confirms human ups and downs, waves of discontent, abundant accomplishment, watershed events, catastrophic failures, and, as noted earlier, the recurring appearance of fascinating men and women who change the world. Find times of war, captivity, division, and unsettledness, and you will find ancestors speaking to us through the ages. Like my grandparents, or my fourth-grade teacher, or the pastor next door, lives and history influence and teach.

What can we learn from the suffering of those enslaved in Egypt before the exodus? What about the courage of American bomber crews in World War II or the tragedy of a Jew confined to Auschwitz in 1943?

Does Jesus' teaching challenge or chastise? What does David's life teach us? What about Paul or Lincoln or Washington or your parents or grandparents or mentors?

Once upon a time, our nation shared many common beliefs. Faith, a strong work ethic, a clear sense of right and wrong, rooting for the underdog, admiration for success, caring for others, and optimism were some of those common beliefs. I realize that no two humans beliefs were ever exactly the same and shouldn't be, but as to matters of national importance, right and wrong and ethics, we were not that far apart. We might have chosen Democrats or Republicans, chocolate or vanilla, but our core values were for the most part very, very similar. Americans asked similar questions and possessed an inherent desire that their children be better educated, healthier, and free from war and strife.

During the late twentieth century, common core values became increasingly irrelevant. With that loss, much of our national uniqueness evaporated; we became much like other parts of the world: conflicted, confused, and aimless. Our institutions began letting us down. Government spent more money than ever, but response to disasters and war seemed difficult, expensive, and overwhelming. Even our historical drive to be the best was questioned as being inappropriate. There are no simple answers here, but let me suggest a consideration. Just after World War II, faith and national confidence exploded; nothing was considered impossible, including putting a man on the moon. Eventually, war, persistent poverty, the highly publicized opinion that "God is dead," soaring divorce rates, economic woes, and an increasingly divided and pluralistic society exacted a great toll. Almost overnight, nothing seemed possible. Our loss of confidence in God and each other adversely affected this nation and our families.

We have certainly lost our confidence before. Read historical accounts of financial panics and wars, and you will easily find many accounts of discouragement, even riots. For a good example, read about the burning of Washington during the War of 1812, followed by Andrew Jackson's great victory in New Orleans. Our difficulties are not unique, not unprecedented, not all that difficult to solve, and not a deterrent to a determined set of new leaders. Unlike our predecessors, we have not yet experienced revolution, pandemics, slavery, and civil war. Despite those occurrences, our ancestors survived, adapted, took care of families, and fostered ideas and concepts that continue to inspire and affect us today. I am sure there were times when quitting seemed to be the only option. Yet here we are; perseverance prevailed despite all of their trials.

Young lives are very capable of replicating lives well lived so that, eventually, similar beliefs and backstories fill those same young lives. This "system restore" or "do over," if you will, comes to life when our confidence in God is restored and when we care enough about others, especially young people, to listen, guide, and love in the troubled times. Unexpected Generation members hunger for defining and guiding voices. Listen to a voice of the ages:

- "I predict future happiness for Americans if they can prevent the government from wasting the labors of the people under the pretense of taking care of them."
- "It is incumbent on every generation to pay its own debts as it goes. A principle which if acted on would save one-half the wars of the world."
- "My reading of history convinces me that most bad government results from too much government."
- "The tree of liberty must be refreshed from time to time with the blood of patriots and tyrants."
- "The spirit of resistance to government is so valuable on certain occasions that I wish it to be always kept alive."
- "Timid men prefer the calm of despotism to the tempestuous sea of liberty."
- "To compel a man to furnish funds for the propagation of ideas he disbelieves and abhors is sinful and tyrannical."
- "When the people fear the government, there is tyranny. When the government fears the people, there is liberty."
- "I am not a friend to a very energetic government. It is always oppressive."
- "History, in general, only informs us of what bad government is."
- "I would rather be exposed to the inconveniences attending too much liberty than to those attending too small a degree of it."
- "Were we directed from Washington when to sow and when to reap, we should soon want bread."
- "The democracy will cease to exist when you take away from those who are willing to work and give to those who would not."

- "I tremble for my country when I reflect that God is just; that his justice cannot sleep forever."

All of these statements are attributed to Thomas Jefferson.

Jefferson was an older-model Unexpected Generation member who knew, peering through the ages, that challenges come and difficulties are always around the corner, but so is human persistence and wisdom born in experience. Jefferson knew someone would one day listen to him, that liberty would one day be jeopardized, and that government would once again become oppressive. John Locke, noted philosopher, had a profound influence on Jefferson. Locke died almost forty years before Jefferson was born, yet Locke's philosophies are clearly found in the Declaration of Independence and many of Jefferson's writings. Jefferson no doubt considered those who had gone on before and those who would follow.

System restores and do overs are simply applied methods of understanding and remembering quality beliefs and lives that preceded our time. Looking back, we once again find heroes, seek out lives and beliefs to admire, and dust off concepts such as liberty and competition. Being unashamed of founding principles and our belief in Jesus Christ are examples. Admiring lives well lived, such as those of William Wilberforce and Martin Luther, suddenly becomes relevant. Concepts become important again, common core values reemerge, and our social fabric heals. The loudest voices do not prevail. Traditions do not become debilitating or controlling. The momentum of failure is stymied. We once again begin asking the questions "Why?" and "Why not?" Our creativity surges, as does our concern for others. We become not products of the last few decades but products of the ages. I know all that sounds too good to be true, and I realize that our forefathers, spiritual and otherwise, had their issues. Future generations were nevertheless worth their blood. We are important to those who follow, and they should be important to us. Do overs matter for those who follow, and occasionally for us too.

I did not realize that my 2010 family vacation would lead to a personal do over. Just as we arrived at the beach, my brother called with troubling news. Dad was in the hospital, facing emergency surgery for a bowel obstruction. There were no options; surgery was a must. "Everything will be fine," my brother said. "Don't come back home. We've got it." The year before, my son had become ill, causing me to fly home on the first day of vacation. Maybe my brother remembered that episode with my son, but my decision to stay with my family came with some apprehension.

Dad came through surgery fine but had trouble waking up. When I arrived a few days later, he was still out of it—no communication whatsoever. Within a few days, he had contracted a MRSA throat infection and, a few days later, deadly MRSA pneumonia. We made the decision to place him on a ventilator, and precautions were necessary just to visit. Dad went downhill very fast. We sensed inevitability as ICU nurses reassured us that there are worse things than death. My brothers and I gathered one Sunday morning for what was expected to be Dad's last day on earth. Dad's testimony was freely shared, and there was no doubt about his final destination. Friends and relatives came to say good-bye to a long-lived, good man. My decision not to be with Dad before surgery was haunting me. I had missed my last opportunity to hug Dad's neck and tell him I loved him. Around noon that Sunday, I stepped out for a rushed bite of lunch and to pray to my heavenly Father.

I know that good outcomes are not always God's will, but this time God provided. God spoke clearly that, against all odds, my dad would live. When I shared that message a few minutes later with my brothers, they wondered where I had gone for lunch and what I had to drink, but they believed soon enough. God gave me another chance with my dad. He is not quite the same after his near-death experience and the onset of dementia, but he knows when I hug his neck and tell him that I love him.

Prior to Dad's illness and during a 2009 trip to Israel mentioned in Chapter 3, I was afforded a time in a unique location to consider second opportunities and do overs. Standing on the north shore of the Sea of Galilee, where a resurrected Jesus called Peter into the ministry, I sensed, despite millennia of separation, Peter's emotional and spiritual upheaval. Hiding tears from my fellow travelers, I flinched at the thought of Peter's denying Christ not once but three times. My tears were also joyful at knowing that a loving, forgiving savior knew exactly what Peter was experiencing and how badly this soon-to-be rock of the church needed reassurance and a second chance.

John 21:15–17 states the following:

15 So when they had dined, Jesus saith to Simon Peter, Simon, son of Jonas, lovest thou me more than these? He saith unto him, Yea, Lord; thou knowest that I love thee. He saith unto him, Feed my lambs.

16 He saith to him again the second time, Simon, [son] of Jonas, lovest thou me? He saith unto him, Yea, Lord; thou knowest that I love thee. He saith unto him, Feed my sheep.

17 He saith unto him the third time, Simon [son] of Jonas, lovest thou me? Peter was grieved because he said unto him the third time, Lovest thou me? And he said unto him, Lord, thou knowest all things; thou knowest that I love thee. Jesus saith unto him, Feed my sheep.

Peter was afforded three opportunities to confirm his love for Christ in response to three earlier denials. The resulting second chance did not result in a life of ease and smooth sailing; Peter would face challenge after challenge and ultimately give his life for the cause of a risen Savior. Peter is a hero and an example that lives can be well lived despite earlier failures and struggles.

Like Peter, and as with my experience with my dad, God is more than ready to give each of us and the United States of America a second chance. Our national system restore is the emergence of the Unexpected Generation. Our do over is the restoration of a nation so unique, so free, and so blessed that history will record an amazing comeback, a turnaround of biblical proportions, and long-awaited heroes who are probably sitting with you at dinner, who are the distant recipients of tuition checks, who are soldiers standing guard in Afghanistan, the clerks at the grocery store, or your waitress at dinner. You might want to leave a big tip. That waitress could be the future president of the United States.

CHAPTER 8

How Hard Can This Be?

A ship in a safe harbor is safe—that is
not what a ship is built for.
—William Shed

My reputation for being "handy" around my home or office is a bit sullied. People literally run in a panic if I so much as pick up a hammer or a bottle of glue. Car windshields have been broken and insurance claims made, and mothers shield small children from the carnage as they retreat, exclaiming loudly, "Oh, the humanity!" Well, maybe it is not quite that bad. I did grow up working in construction, and at age ten or so, I fashioned myself quite the mechanic. Near that time, Dad bought a brand new Snapper Comet riding lawn mower, the same riding mower Forrest Gump used. As a ten-year-old anxious to drive anything, nothing was more exciting than the acquisition of that shiny red mower. Modifications were inevitable, so a much-needed muffler was soon replaced by a straight metal pipe. The sound was deafening. Neighbors nevertheless hired me to cut their grass, and at three dollars per lawn, I was soon in the money. With my newfound wealth, I bought baseball gloves, shotgun shells, and some clothing.

There was even enough money to rent a motorcycle for an hour while on vacation at Panama City, Florida. There was a rather significant problem with that rental. I didn't have a driver's license, and the account of my near arrest for that little episode is another story for another day.

Before the hot rod Snapper Comet, we owned a sporadically running push mower. Seeking to make my dad proud, I sought solutions to end the beast's foul habits once and for all. My inquiring ten-year-old mind soon determined that if I held the "butterfly" of the carburetor open, the mower ran. I considered different methods to fix the problem and eventually determined that one of my mother's spools of thread would fit perfectly into the carburetor, which then allowed me to tie the carburetor butterfly into the open position. Believe it or not, this brilliant plan worked. The lawn mower ran like a sewing machine! (Sorry.) Well, at least for a while. Eventually, the mower returned to its old habits, running poorly, if at all. A trip to a real mechanic followed, as did I.

I was fascinated by the chaotic jumble of a small engine repair shop where, in the waning hours of a sweet spring day, I inhaled and savored the complex odors of oil, grease, and gasoline. Fellow travelers drawn to this odiferous mecca chatted and visited while subtly hiding and denying the shame of overgrown lawns. The mechanic, a tall man with an air of infinite patience, rightly assumed the carburetor was our problem. Here was a man worthy of this project, wise and skilled. I wondered if he would admire my innovative carburetor solution.

"No wonder this thing won't work!" he said. "I've never seen anything like this. Some idiot put a spool of thread in the carburetor. Who in the world put a spool of thread in a carburetor?" I think there might have even been an expletive or two woven into the conversation. The excitement attracted not only my dad but many other visitors to the repair shop, who suddenly were analyzing one of the great mysteries of the modern world: Where had that spool of thread come from? The repair shop was suddenly not as interesting. I was ready to go home, red faced, nervous, and hopeful that no one would even offer a guess that I was the likely culprit.

Traumatized and embarrassed, I told no one of my secret. The spool of thread remained a mystery for almost fifty years. Recently I shared this story with my family and my staff. I guess confession was good for the soul, but suddenly I realized that I had suppressed the mechanic's question for a very long time. What if I had answered way back then? Would I have been ridiculed in front of the crowd or commended for at least trying something new? Who knows?

The point of my lawn mower story is blatant. There are some questions we hope are never asked and some we hope to never answer. Those annoying questions are problematic, though. If we never ask or answer uncomfortable questions, if we hide or live in denial, what happens? The last fifty years happens, and that time period has not been especially kind to our country, churches, and families.

Uncomfortable questions teach us never to place spools of thread in carburetors. Uncomfortable answers force us to reflect, to consider, and to hopefully improve ourselves. We become more willing to seek help, to undertake self-help, and to weather the inevitable ridicule and hurt that life doles out in excess. I might have been embarrassed to answer the mechanic, but if I had justified my reasoning, he might have been impressed. The carburetor might have been fixed sooner and with less expense. The assembled crowd might have had a laugh and poked a little fun at me, and they might have remembered a goofy kid that tried to fix lawn mowers and did society a favor by attending law school. They may have remembered a spring evening in a lawn mower shop when a boy told the truth, took his medicine, and took it like a man. That memory might have caused them to hire me one day.

We learn from questions posed and answered every day. Some questions and answers are mundane components of our work and home lives. But some questions and answers are gifts from God that may at first seem painful or unsettling. Those questions and answers challenge our behavior and our relationships, and not many of us like challenge or change. The one offering those questions and answers wants nothing but what is best for us. Our humanity, my humanity, shows up in my lawn mower shop experience. Often we run, deny, and delay when questions or answers are inconvenient or difficult or actually require a course change. Denial and avoidance of God's questions and answers come with a very high price. God is not necessarily punishing us for dodging his Q&A session. Quite the contrary, we simply experience the consequences of ignoring his danger warnings. And when we experience those consequences, we may pose more questions to God than ourselves. Why is this happening? Where is God? Why me? Why now? Why? Contrast those questions to the following: What opportunities is God providing? Where have I been? Why not me? Why not now? Why not? _Do we not hide behind wrong questions and answers?_ Remember, King Saul hid behind the baggage just before his call to be king.

20 And when Samuel had caused all the tribes of Israel to come near, the tribe of Benjamin was taken.

21 When he had caused the tribe of Benjamin to come near by their families, the family of Matri was taken, and Saul the son of Kish was taken: and when they sought him, he could not be found.

22 Therefore they enquired of the LORD further, if the man should yet come thither. And the LORD answered, Behold he hath hid himself among the stuff. (1 Sam. 10:20–22)

The "stuff" of life will not hide us from God's questions. After I came out from the "stuff," I remembered a valuable but belated lawn mower shop lesson, which is simply this: face questions and problems head on; don't let the circumstances or those present define me or my ethics; don't hide, run, or deny. Tell the truth, even when it hurts. If I had followed every one of those lessons throughout my life, I would have avoided many problems and much pain.

When God's questions are considered, when we seek a higher level of living, when we are candid with ourselves and others, tough questions and answers have profound meaning and consequence. You will without question be separated from those too afraid to ask or answer. Courageous questions and answers invigorate our relationship with our heavenly Father. Spiritual numbness exits. Expect reappearance of fascination and exuberance and the exit of darkness and forlornness. Inhibitions evaporate, boldness appears, and we become much more aware of blessings and fellow travelers, like Unexpected Generation members. Expecting the unexpected brings us closer to the "zone" where God wants us to be. I did not say "comfort zone," though.

God frequently calls me from my comfort zone, and I expect he does the same with you. I can assure you that some of those experiences required all the faith I am able to muster. Yet they also offered some of the sweetest times of my life, when God's promise and protection became visible, when his plan for my life became tangible, and when his marvelous grace became simultaneously real yet inexplicable with mortal tongue. Those experiences have also offered an opportunity to comfort and encourage others facing similar journeys.

There are certainly questions during God's call to "go here" or "do this," but oddly, not that many. In advance of God's calling or when I was out of his will, I had many more questions. I remember some of those questions: "What am I doing?" "Is this where I am supposed to be?" You may be experiencing one of those times of questioning everything. Answers may be few. You may be angry with God, doubting, unsure, and maybe not all that pleasant to be around. Been there Done it. Understand. Let me offer one question you must ultimately ask, a question that puts all in perspective and that you should clearly think about and pray about before asking. This, in fact, may be the most annoying, scariest, most dangerous, most radical question not only in this writing but in the world. That question is simply this: *"God, what may I do for you?"* If you are courageous enough to ask that question, are you courageous enough to listen when he answers? Patient enough? Faithful enough? Willing enough? Trusting enough? If you do not know Jesus Christ as your savior, are you willing enough to trust him with your eternity? Would you leave on a mission trip tomorrow, forsaking family, job, wealth, and safety on an answer flowing from an unseen being, speaking to you after you asked a very simple question? Is God speaking to you right now? Is it time to rededicate? Is it finally time to care about what God has in store for you and your family? Is there anything hindering you, holding you back, or frightening you? What will you do about that tangled spool of thread clogging your spiritual carburetor?

My goal for the remainder of this writing is simply to pose fast-paced, tough questions that challenge you to think, to understand, to study, to prepare, to participate, and to help those who will soon change the world. Tough questions allow you to think like Unexpected Generation members. Do not let your political affiliations, personal history, and preconceptions control. Take time to reason; think like you never have before. Be creative. The more outrageous the answer, the more likely it is that you are on to something. There is no rush to read this little book of annoying questions. Despite the intentional brevity of this writing, your thoughtful consideration of questions posed will absolutely take some time, and reading may take longer than anticipated.

Questions are first directed to each of us, to be followed by questions to our society. At risk of some overlap, I believe there are some important distinctions. Questions posed to religious organizations are very necessary but also very painful. You have likely realized that I look forward to questions posed to our government.

Consider the following difficult-to-attribute statement before we begin some difficult questioning "If everyone would see to his own reformation, how very easily you might reform a nation."

ANNOYING QUESTIONS DIRECTED AT US

Which of the following is most important to you: wealth, beauty, freedom, or your relationship with God? What does that choice say about you? Is that really your choice, or did that choice just sound good? Does television define your expectation of wealth, beauty, freedom, or faith? Are you an independent thinker? Is it more important to get along than to confront? Why is it so much easier to see your neighbor's faults rather than your own? How would you grade yourself as a son or daughter, a parent, a citizen, a human being? Do you have any desire to be a better person? How do you define better? If you are a parent or grandparent, do you have a concern for the next generation? What are you willing to give up to benefit your nation and your descendants? Anything? Do you feel entitled to anything? Do you look at the big picture? Do you look at the short term and the long term? Are you scared? Concerned? Motivated? Ready for change? Prepared for change? Are you willing to support new, innovative leaders who will pose difficult questions and implement difficult solutions? What if that costs you money? What if that decision affects your personal comfort?

Do you know who your children's teachers are? Have you read any of your children's textbooks? Are you aware of what is being taught? Are there potentially damaging agendas being taught to impressionable minds?

73

Last year my wife began mentoring a nine-year-old girl who immediately became part of our family. Fascinated with computers, Justin Bieber, and our cell phones, this smart, fun-loving young lady struggled occasionally at home and at school. I love baseball, so my children grew up playing catch for most of their young lives. Our mentee had never experienced anyone taking time to play catch or take batting practice with her. A little time in the front yard revealed some talent. She was quite a hitter. I won't go into all the details about this young lady's life, but suffice it to say that she has endured more than any nine-year-old should. I would venture that an hour in the hot sun throwing and batting a few softballs will be remembered by both of us for a long, long time. Have you thrown a ball with a kid in recent memory?

Dads, why have so many of you abandoned your children? Where have you been? Do you realize that you have only one shot at being Dad?

For those of you involved in your family's lives, do you ever talk to your children about sacrifice? What about character or integrity? Have you been a good example or bad example? Could you explain hard work and patience to your children? What about perseverance? Can you think of anyone in history who persevered and succeeded? Failed? Do you tell family stories to your children or grandchildren? Do you share meals with them? Do you really inquire about what is going on in their lives?

Have you ever taken your children to church or a place of worship? Are you just going through the motions in your worship if you even worship at all? Do you talk to your children about faith? What about personal responsibility? Have you been responsible? Are you disciplined? Have you ever discussed or taught concern for others? Have you ever mentioned honesty?

Would you give up freedom for security? *Is any idea, any thought, any concept more important than you and your family?*

Have you ever visited a battlefield or a museum? Did you take your children or your grandchildren? Did you talk about men and women dying for beliefs?

How much television do you watch? What was the last book you read? The last class you attended? Do you have any desire to improve yourself or your family? Are you content where you are as a person? Do you have any goal other than retirement, obtaining more possessions, or making more money?

When was the last time you helped somebody who was down on their luck?

As I wrote these long lists of questions, events occurred that prompted another question. Serving alongside an Army recruiter at a homeless mission, I noticed that selfless soldier literally remove his own shirt and give it to a homeless man. This faithful servant grew up in the Ninth Ward of New Orleans, where temptations and lifestyles could and did take a toll on a young man. But God intervened in his life, pulling him from the risks of his hometown and allowing a career as a soldier. That life led to war and injuries, but his most difficult battle of late is with his wife's breast cancer. I recently overheard his sharing a moment of encouragement and compassion with a struggling soul. His message was clear: God is ever present in times of trouble. I think you will now understand the next question.

Would you give the shirt off your back to someone in need?

Whom do you admire most? Do you believe in anything eternal? In yourself?

Do you work? If not, why not? Would you like more education?

Have you ever read the Bible? Will you?

Do you return your grocery cart to the cart return? If you do, will you do the same on a cold rainy night? What do those actions say about you?

To what extent will you go to avoid risk? Are you willing to encounter criticism for your beliefs? Are you able to communicate three of your most important beliefs?

Are you addicted to anything? Are you able to end that addiction? Will you reach out for help? When?

Have you ever taken time to watch the sun rise or set? Have you ever sat on a beach or played in the ocean surf? Ever watched a thunderstorm just for the wonder of it? Were you amazed at the birth of a child? Have you ever inspired a young person? Have you ever inspired anyone? Do not young people hunger for heroes? For caring relationships? For someone to confide in? Any chance a young person would seek you out for help? Why or why not?

If you died today, would anyone care? Who would come to your funeral? Would they mourn or rejoice?

What is on your "bucket list"?

Do you believe we are spiritual beings? Do you believe in heaven? Angels? Jesus Christ? Have you ever had a calling to do something? Did you do it?

Are you just trying to recapture something in your life? Is that search all about your youth? Missed opportunities?

Has anyone told you they appreciated you? Admired you? Loved you? Are you searching for someone to love you? Any luck? Does anyone really understand you?

Have you ever forgiven someone? Have you ever been forgiven? What condition in your life defines you more than any other? Is that a proper definition of you? Is anyone else defining you? Do you believe we all have souls? Do you believe we are all unique? Does your individuality matter to anyone? Does it matter to you? Have you accomplished anything that you have been proud of? Recently?

Have you ever accepted responsibility for your actions? Have you ever accepted responsibility even when you were not at fault?

Do you ridicule anyone for their faith? Their beliefs? Have you been ridiculed for either of those reasons? How did that feel?

Do you protect your children from all possible harm? Are you a "helicopter parent," hovering over your children? Should not a young person experience heartbreak and pain to learn?

Do you envy the wealth of others? Why? Do you long for similar success? Would you harm or take anything from someone simply because they had more wealth?

Are you content? Do you like to see others succeed, or does that bother you? If you are bothered, who taught you to be bothered? Were they right? Are you defined by what you don't have? Are you jealous of anyone? Do you admire what someone has accomplished or what they have? Have you ever examined what made someone successful?

Is your income dependent upon a government check? Have you ever saved anything? What is your most precious possession outside of family members? What would you carry out first from your burning home?

What is your favorite season? Your favorite childhood memory? The most influential person in your life? Who were your favorite teachers?

What is your favorite adult memory? What last took your breath away? Have your ever stood on a mountain peak at dawn? Do you contemplate anything beyond the next meal?

I know those questions are annoying. Unexpected Generation members will pose many, many more.

CHAPTER 9

Can You Play at the Next Level?

*If we are growing, we're always going
to be out of our comfort zone.*
—John Maxwell

In 2007, my son briefly attended a small college in Birmingham, Alabama, to play football. His college team played some initial games at storied Legion Field in downtown Birmingham. Running late for one of his games and in total reliance on my GPS, I exited I-65 and followed a previously untaken route to the stadium. Within moments, the excitement of attending a football game was replaced with sadness and heartbreak. The GPS route change carried us through a portion of Birmingham that, to be honest, was third world. Decay, hopelessness, barred windows and doors, and poverty became very evident. The contrast between my home and this community was stark. I have been blessed to own a good house in a safe, stable neighborhood. Why me? Why was I not a child from that community in Birmingham, a community where shootings were routine and lives were shortened by strife, heartache, and division? I had asked that question before. Why was I born in the United States with every opportunity and someone else was born in Afghanistan or in China in poverty and suppression? Why was I brought up to attend church and to love God, family, and country? Why should I be saved by the grace of God through Jesus Christ? Grace and salvation cannot be just for the lucky, can it?

Luke 12:48 states, in part, "For unto whomsoever much is given, of him shall be much required: and to whom men have committed much, of him they will ask the more."

For most of my adult life, I have listened to and quoted this Scripture at convenient times. Honestly, I did not pay that much attention to the last phrase. Quoting Scripture out of context can lead to false doctrine, a danger among many of our faithful. Considering that phrase reminded me that service really never ends. There is little time to rest because the more we do; the more we have to do. Understand there are limits, but are those our motivational limits or our physical limits? If we are motivated and guided by the Holy Spirit, our potential is unlimited. And when we open ourselves to unrestrained service, those families and children in downtown Birmingham, Afghanistan, China, and other places of great need will hear of Christ. The Great Commission in Matthew 28:18–20 states the following:

18 And Jesus came and spake unto them, saying, All power is given unto me in heaven and in earth.

19 Go ye therefore, and teach all nations, baptizing them in the name of the Father, and of the Son, and of the Holy Ghost:

20 Teaching them to observe all things whatsoever I have commanded you: and, lo, I am with you always, [even] unto the end of the world. Amen.

We love verse 20 because of its reassurance, but verse 19 is not so comforting. We are uncomfortable being told that there are no boundaries to our missions. We are to teach all nations, not just the convenient ones. Understanding that Christ has all power to help us and that he will never leave us alone should result in incredible boldness and motivation, but asking for bold missions regardless of our finances, our families, our jobs, our physical conditions, and our confidence in the Word of God scares us silly. We understand that God may take us up on our tepid offers of service such that we lose control over where we live and how we make a living. That loss of control, that submission to God's will, is unfortunately undertaken by very few. We plan and live as though we are in control. We may save and buy into the commercials of sun-soaked retirement without a care in the world, but God may well have a different plan.

If we are afraid to go, teach, and baptize, should we wonder why our churches are aging and shrinking and why Christianity means less and less to Millennials and much of the world? As a wise person once told me, "We do what we want to do."

My experience in Birmingham challenged me. What mission had I undertaken? Did I care about anyone who was inconvenient to care for? Had I just shared a little with a family down on its luck at Christmas and then considered that effort adequate until the next Christmas? Maybe I had given a little time to a church or charity and considered that feeble effort adequate, too. Had I comforted myself that my work and service was limited to attending church on Sunday, contributing to the collection plate, comforting church members during times of loss, and not much else? Had I done anything worthwhile in over a half a century of living? Had I simply taken up space?

We joke about relevance when we ask, "What have you done for me lately?" Just before my Birmingham experience, I was at risk of being absorbed in work and my son's football career. I had forgotten my most important service. Confronting shortcomings is not pleasant, and my

Birmingham experience shook me up. Was my heavy heart a challenge or a condemnation? What would I do about either?

I can assure you that I did not enjoy my son's football game on what was otherwise a beautiful fall afternoon. Questions raced through my mind: How did we get here as a nation? Should inhabitants of those houses assume personal responsibility for better conditions, or did they need help? Were they perfectly happy with their conditions? Was I a potential meddler? Do we really live in a great nation when some are afraid and captive behind barred windows? How many other cities had conditions just the same or worse than Birmingham? What about educational opportunities? How good were their schools? Did anybody really want out? What could I do?

I shared my eye-opening experience with others, and soon realized that God places different concerns on the hearts of different people. Honestly, no one was interested in serving a community over one hundred miles away. I began asking what business I had telling people I didn't know what to do in their community. What about problems closer to home? Had I become burdened with a problem that had no answer? Perhaps. Perhaps our inability to find answers is the very reason those communities are rotting off the face of the planet and taking many lives in the process.

Eventually I moved on, trying to deal with the Great Recession and taking care of my family, but each trip through a rough part of town painfully reminded me of that fall Saturday in Birmingham and my inadequacies. I often speak to young people about changing the world, and I realized that my role in world changing was limited to an increase in room temperature caused solely by hot air exiting my mouth. My legacy of shallow platitudes and words lasted no longer than my speeches. James 2:17 is very clear: Faith without works is dead.

God occasionally provides unexpected gifts at unexpected times. Two years of ignoring conditions in tired communities came to an abrupt end when I met my friend Pastor Clifton Dawkins. Dawkins serves as the Fulton County, Georgia, chaplain and says final words over some four hundred-plus indigent burials each year. Some of those poor souls are known only to God, but Dawkins offers the dignity of someone caring. He also feeds more than three hundred homeless folks in downtown Atlanta every Saturday morning. Clifton's tiny church often struggles to pay bills and keep the doors open. This good man came into my life asking for some help among a large group of Baptists gathered for a meeting. Within a few days, I was serving food to homeless folks in a parking lot near the City of Atlanta Jail. Nothing sheltered us from the elements, and nothing sheltered my apprehension. Despite my efforts to move on with life, God had not forgotten my Birmingham burden.

Some in the food line were mere boys. One young man appeared out of place. He had that wiry, intense look of an athlete, one I would have loved to coach in youth baseball or basketball. He would soon change my life.

"You play ball?" I inquired. He lit up—yes, he played basketball. "Coach thought I could play at the next level," he said. You can tell when someone is reminded of a failure, of loss in his life. That young man never made it to the next level. Something went wrong, and now he was on the streets, hungry and homeless. He may have been talented, but any outlet for that talent was now gone and the replacements were not all that attractive. Instead of playing basketball, this young man was now focused on finding shelter and a meal—basic human subsistence. He had a nickname: NBA. He would haunt me on cold nights that followed as I wondered if he was fed and warm.

NBA also haunted me for another reason. Had I gone to the next level? My answer was, clearly, no. I was capable of so much more, and I had failed miserably. So many needs, lost souls, and incredible potential, and I had been oblivious to it all. And worse, most of the churches in my area were just as clueless.

As I returned downtown to help feed homeless during the Christmas season, for some reason I was burdened to make a stop at a Wal-Mart near my home. There I would buy a little Christmas treat for as many homeless folks as possible. A little chocolate or sweet might make someone's day or allow me to offer a moment of conversation and encouragement. With NBA on my heart, I purchased a basketball, a gift bag and a Christmas card. Inside I wrote, "Time for the next level, son." That note was as much to me as to NBA.

I anxiously awaited NBA's return to the food line, but much to my disappointment, he didn't show. I handed the gift to Pastor Dawkins and asked that he give the basketball to NBA next time he showed up. Sad that I couldn't share my gift, I left. A few minutes later, Pastor Dawkins called. NBA had shown up late, and the basketball and note were delivered.

All the frustration of the Birmingham experience immediately departed in a moment of unspeakable joy. I may not have been able to rebuild a troubled neighborhood with bricks and mortar, but the prospect of blessing and encouraging someone, of helping with a first step to rebuild one life, blew me away. I wondered how many lives could be changed if someone like my grandparents or a mechanic or a teacher took a moment to care and to encourage someone who was down on his luck. While my journey from Birmingham to Atlanta was slightly over a hundred miles, the real journey was much longer and much more challenging. Giving a basketball to someone on a cold winter's day is not a solution to a problem. Understanding that our time in this world is limited jolts us away from complacency, though. We need to matter. We need to matter for God. And we need to matter soon.

A more complex personal journey included a question as to whether I had changed how I loved and cared for those of a different color, economic status, and education. Had I discovered how Jesus loved tax collectors, prostitutes, and those rejected by the Pharisees? Does any of that care and love make a difference to someone hungry and freezing to death? Do we have lost and troubled souls on our hearts, or are they just inconvenient? Are we reliant upon God to help us find opportunities to serve? Will we recognize those opportunities? Will we act?

The journey and the questions continue, but my life did change. I enjoy every opportunity to help homeless and hungry folks. After sharing my experiences with pastors, churches, and even graduate programs at major universities, hundreds have joined Pastor Dawkins to serve the needy, not because of me but because our loving heavenly Father wants us to live on the "next level." God provided opportunities, willing hearts, and workers. I never saw NBA again. He may well be on those streets, cold and hungry, but I like to imagine that God worked in his life too, challenging him as he did me to undertake his full potential. I pray that is the case, but NBA was followed by an older man in need of reading glasses, and then shoes, and a man named Bobby who just wanted a good pillow, who was followed by a long line of souls and needs, including one sweet lady who needed something much more important.

One of my childhood friends pastors a church near my home. His heart is as big as Atlanta, so I was not surprised when he quickly connected with a lady in trouble while working at a Saturday homeless meal. After sharing the Gospel, my friend was able to lead that lady to a joyful and emotional acceptance of Jesus Christ as her savior. If my journey from Birmingham resulted in nothing more than observing that lady's salvation, then I count myself highly favored among men. Others serving food nearby heard the good news and quickly rejoiced, much like I had with the NBA experience. Later that same day, young men and women representing churches from my community joined with homeless men and women in an exuberant line dance. I am not kidding. I laughed before realizing that I was capturing a glimpse of eternity, where our joy will never end, where no one will be judged, cold, hungry, or ill-clothed. I have hugged dirty homeless folks, loved them, prayed with them, attended church several times in an African-American community, sung, rejoiced, and been eternally blessed by the simple step of buying a basketball and a Christmas card for someone I barely knew and because God and a GPS carried me on a route that I would never have taken. That route allowed me to become aware of ministries never before considered, of spiritual risk taking, of sharing needs like never before. There are abundant ministries in jails, retirement homes, ball fields, hospitals, and countless other locations for the observant and those pursuing an "entrepreneurial faith."

Are you talking a good game or playing one? When we burn away the tinder and debris covering our hearts and eyes, does not something wonderful happen?

Unexpected Generation members are ready to challenge our complacency and inaction. Unlike me, they will assume Birmingham is their home turf as they challenge third-world living standards. They will not waste almost half a century with inaction as I did.

ANNOYING QUESTIONS DIRECTED AT OUR SOCIETY

Are we ready to join Unexpected Generation members and live on the "next level"? Does fear ever enter into that question? Does the "next level" occur only when we open our hearts or also when we unconditionally forgive one another? Why is forgiveness so important?

So difficult? Why do we harbor grudges, jealousies, and divisions, some based entirely on ancestors and events that are centuries old? How relevant are those divisions and hatreds? Do we just enjoy the fight, or is it convenient to blame others for our circumstances? Wouldn't moving on be refreshing and take less energy?

Does "moral" matter? How do we define *moral?*

Do we live in denial of needs all around us? Are we happy to live in our own little worlds, content, clueless, and never really making a difference? Are we afraid to go where the needs are? Do we struggle with the "why me" question?

We may be all endowed with equality, but are we really equally endowed? If not, should we expect the same callings, blessings, service, and results? Are not some meant to be plumbers and some doctors? Is everyone supposed to go to college? Who will dig our ditches? Do we condescend to any profession? Are we not all valuable?

Recently I met Mary Frances Bowley with Wellspring Living. Wellspring is an organization committed to rescuing young ladies who are trapped in the sex trade. Mary Frances and others like her routinely and boldly intervene so as to save lives from addictions, abuse, and exploitation. I had no awareness of this serious issue before meeting Mary Frances. Her organization, with God's help, has transformed many lives, but the need is overwhelming and unfortunately worldwide. The following questions should remind us that someone's daughter is in danger every day.

When do we look at women as something other than a commodity? Are not all women God's creations? Are they not someone's daughters? Are they not precious to someone, somewhere? Would you ever consider a rescue and intervention for someone involved in prostitution? Would you stand up to a pimp to save a young lady?

Why does human trafficking exist in our society? Is that not slavery?

When do children become precious again? Who would exploit or harm a child? What does that say about our society? Why does pornography, especially child pornography, have any market? What decent person could tolerate the emotional and physical abuse of a child?

Why do we not let little boys be little boys? Why are American men under attack? Do they deserve it?

Do we value life, or has life been cheapened? Why do young men die in our streets for no good reason? Why do some value cats, dogs, and trees over children and other human beings?

Do you believe all cultures are valuable? If not, when do we have enough guts to condemn cultures that are evil and inferior in their treatment of women, children, and others? How do we recover souls from evil cultures? Who is strong enough and righteous enough to condemn evil cultures? Who among us can take the heat and criticism when doing so?

Last year my sons' former roommate died of an overdose. A bright, talented, funny, promising young man's life ended, despite intervention. My heart still breaks over that loss, which will forever affect my family. An opportunity to counsel needy people recently allowed me to meet a beautiful young lady who struggled with an addiction to crystal meth. Her desperate plea for help, for someone to release her from her dark prison of addiction, shook my being. She shared awful dreams of death and separation, dreams that hopefully never become reality. Three weeks of sobriety gave her some hope, but I sensed the turmoil of her torn soul.

Why do so many numb themselves with drugs? Is life ever that bad? How many homes and families have been destroyed by drugs and alcohol? Why have all of our efforts to combat drug addiction failed for the most part? Why do young people become addicted every day despite having good parents and grandparents and many people who care about them? What are you addicted to? What are your plans to become sober and free again?

How do we treat our senior citizens? When did you last talk to an older American? Did you listen to his or her story? If you listened, did the story scare or inspire you? Did that story mean anything to you? Do we admire their accomplishments, or are they just a burden to us?

Why are celebrities so important to us? Do you read the tabloids or watch the celebrity news on television? Are those celebrities your heroes, good examples, bad examples, definition to your life, or totally irrelevant? Do we know how to define a hero versus a celebrity? Would that definition include a teacher, firefighter, soldier, policeman, grandparent, parent, preacher, politician, or missionary?

What criteria do you use to analyze complicated issues? Are your considerations long term, spiritual, moral, balanced, filled with reason, and cognizant of generational affects and costs or just emotional and self-focused reactions?

Is it possible to be really, really honest with each other? No holds barred, free of societal spin and convention, dead level, politically incorrect honest? Do we really want to be that honest? How many people would die if we were that honest? How many people will die if we are not that honest?

What are you afraid to think or ask? What opinion are you afraid to voice?

Do you think of your children and grandchildren when you vote or voice an opinion? Is your opinion or question worth your life?

Do our leaders have to always be articulate? Good looking? Charismatic? Is there something deeper than oratory skills and looks that we should be considering? Are we as shallow as our leaders? Are you capable of recognizing a leader?

Why is it so difficult to trust anyone? Why is it necessary to be so skeptical?

Why are so many predators among us? Why do crooks spend so much time scheming instead of working?

Do we value a good work ethic? Are some just happy to get by?

Are you truly ready for the "next level"? When? Have you taken a shot at getting there? The clock is counting down.

CHAPTER 10

Is Anything Sacred?

When one door closes, another opens; but we often
look so long and so regretfully upon the closed door
that we do not see the other one which has opened.
—Alexander Graham Bell

Growing up in a small, evangelical church in North Georgia, I
attended revival meetings each July, along with Sunday school and
church services every Sunday, all of my life. I was ordained as a deacon,
which is a lifelong commitment to small churches in my community.
In 2010 at age fifty-five, I became concerned about the mission,
outreach, and external service of both my church and several churches
banded together in a local association. I prayed about this concern,
and while on vacation that summer, God provided a stern message, a
message I did not relish bringing to an organization steeped in tradition
and over 170 years of history. In September 2010, I addressed the
association of churches with a God-given message calling for relevance
to the community, enhanced missions, outreach, and a call to abandon
traditions hampering our service. I knew the message was difficult; I
struggled to gain enough courage to stand and certainly realized that
I would lose some relationships and respect for sharing what God had

placed on my heart. In fact, one participating church walked out during my speech. Many others embraced the message and called or sent encouraging notes for months to come. But to some, I was now dead, an enemy and an anathema. As a lawyer, I don't mind confronting wrongs, but to do so in a church environment is to walk through a minefield. To do so among lifelong friends whom I loved and still love today is even more dangerous. I had stepped on many mines, but my calling was so strong that I repeated the same effort in my church. There, strategic planning sessions arranged to discuss changing the worship service format and opening our doors and hearts to missions and discipleship training became painful confrontations focused on which version of the Bible to use, what music was appropriate, and an inordinate concern over what other churches thought about us. Bottom line—the initiative largely failed. I failed.

Eventually, painfully, and probably much to the relief of some, I was led by the Holy Spirit to leave my church, not because of my failure but because God had something else in store for my life. That change in direction was sudden, clear, and dramatic. I am no quitter, but when God says "Go," I go.

During the many long and sleepless nights that followed, I often wondered if I had I handled my God-called mission properly. Did I possess enough patience, love, tolerance, and forgiveness to answer God's call, or had I just become frustrated and disillusioned only to find myself isolated? After leaving, I often vacillated between freedom and heartbreak, regret and loneliness, and finally arrived at resignation to God's plan for my life, whatever that might be. Giving up a physical and spiritual place tied to my youth and my family hurt deeply. Giving up worship with sweet souls who still hug my neck and long for my return was very, very difficult. But when God leads, healing and direction will follow. With God's help, anger subsides; we deal with our circumstances and move on. I will note a much better understanding of Elijah's time under the juniper tree, though.

Missing worship services, I soon began visiting other churches—small, medium, and large with orchestras and choirs or modern music, some with fifty-year old hymnals, some with many young couples or very gray congregations, some with massive mission projects or without any mission at all, some African-American congregations where moving messages and music inspired, others with few members and big buildings, some with big congregations and small buildings, all interesting, all welcoming, and all purposeful. God had given me a new mission, at least for a while, to observe and determine what worked and what didn't in churches of all sizes and demographics. When pastors heard of my journey, some began asking questions: What are you observing? What can you share with us? Realizing my rather enigmatic role, I began making notes and critiques to share with others and perhaps even use in whatever church God calls me to serve with in the future. I eventually found great joy and liberty in visiting different churches even though, as of the conclusion of this writing, I have not joined another church. My separation calmed my old church, offered some guidance to existing churches, and may well lead to a church being planted in God's due time.

If I needed further assurance in a difficult time, another Old Testament hero came through. A brief portion of Joseph's story is found in Genesis 45:1–8.

1   Then Joseph could not refrain himself before all them that stood by him; and he cried, Cause every man to go out from me. And there stood no man with him, while Joseph made himself known unto his brethren.

2   And he wept aloud: and the Egyptians and the house of Pharaoh heard.

3   And Joseph said unto his brethren, I am Joseph; doth my father yet live? And his brethren could not answer him; for they were troubled at his presence.

4   And Joseph said unto his brethren, Come near to me, I pray you. And they came near. And he said, I am Joseph your brother, whom ye sold into Egypt.

5   Now therefore be not grieved, nor angry with yourselves, that ye sold me hither: for God did send me before you to preserve life.

6   For these two years hath the famine been in the land: and yet there are five years, in the which there shall neither be earing nor harvest.

7   And God sent me before you to preserve you a posterity in the earth, and to save your lives by a great deliverance.

8   So now it was not you that sent me hither, but God: and he hath made me a father to Pharaoh, and lord of all his house, and a ruler throughout all the land of Egypt.

Sold into slavery by his brothers, Joseph eventually confronted those brothers during a great famine, having risen to second-in-command of Egypt. Joseph could have immediately jailed his very fearful brothers or sold them into slavery. Who would have blamed him? After being sold, after slavery, after false accusations, and after imprisonment, Joseph possessed not one ounce of bitterness or anger. Realizing God's plan had placed him in each of those terrible situations for a purpose—a purpose being fulfilled by saving much of the known world from starvation—Joseph was sincerely thankful for his journey. That thankfulness turned into forgiveness and, surprisingly, love and compassion for his brothers. Their restored relationship became one of the ultimate do overs. Joseph, the dreamer and preserver, had become dependent on God, spiritually mature, wise, and so plugged into the perfect love of God that his brothers struggled to understand how this could be. Joseph's story is not only a picture of Christ but also of a church defined not by buildings but by love found only through God and his Son. God's love does the unexpected, is exceptional, and floods the world with mercy, forgiveness, and restoration. Joseph's story helped me understand that my stories, including leaving my church, taking walks around Washington, getting a fish hook in my ear, and making emotional visits to downtown Birmingham, are experiences God uses to teach much-needed humility, maturity, and wisdom. Those experiences always send me into the arms of a loving Savior intent on sharing the message of the cross. That message of sacrifice, inexplicable grace, forgiveness, and restoration is powerful, life altering, and irresistible. I cannot help being constantly inspired and amazed.

Eventually I realized how much I had been blessed in attending one church for most of my life. Recalling my baptism on a cloudy July morning and hugging my grandmother and telling her I loved her in the "Awomen" corner of my old church are precious memories that will be carried into eternity. I am not Joseph by any means, but his example helped during a rough time. My brothers and sisters in Christ serving in that association or in my old church remain precious to me. I now know that God is calling me to another mission and that every experience and heartbreak will have purpose at the appropriate time and place. Those experiences are not accidental at all. We are all being daily prepared for our own "next level." From that perspective, I cannot tolerate bitterness, only excitement about what my heavenly Father has in store.

I will note that God did not break when I asked questions. Some relationships did. Some conventions did. Lessons and blessings discovered in times of separation, loneliness, reflection, prayer, and solitude have been more life altering and inspirational than I could ever have imagined.

Months after my church separation, I realized that other lessons were being taught. Even with my professional training and perspective, to some extent I had allowed others and their expectations, not God, to define my path. Breaking free of traditions and expectations affecting my worship and relationship with God was one of the most enlightening spiritual moments of my life. Please understand, I am not advocating a free-for-all in our churches. To do so would result in chaotic and ineffective service to the Lord. However, awareness that God does and will call some to serve differently is vital. Those so called should be accommodated and encouraged instead of being judged and drummed out. There are, of course, doctrinal boundaries, and I realize that some Christians just cannot handle change, but if the Holy Spirit leads one to sing a new song or worship in a different manner, why should anyone object?

I love the story of Gamaliel found in Acts 5. Peter and the other apostles had been jailed and threatened for preaching the Gospel at the temple. Hauled before the Sanhedrin with the very real possibility of getting a death sentence, Peter and the apostles boldly replied, in Acts 5:29, "We ought to obey God rather than men." Incensed, the Sanhedrin considered how to murder Peter and the apostles. Gamaliel—a member of the Sanhedrin, a Pharisee, a lawyer, Paul's teacher, and someone with a reputation for wisdom and teaching abilities—took the stage. Gamaliel likely did not support the apostles, but he did fear that riots would erupt if the popular apostles were harmed. Those riots would have been followed by predictable Roman reprisals. Acts 5:34–39 states the following:

> 34 Then stood there up one in the council, a Pharisee, named Gamaliel, a doctor of the law, had in reputation among all the people, and commanded to put the apostles forth a little space;

35 And said unto them, Ye men of Israel, take heed to yourselves what ye intend to do as touching these men.

36 For before these days rose up Theudas, boasting himself to be somebody; to whom a number of men, about four hundred, joined themselves: who was slain; and all, as many as obeyed him, were scattered, and brought to nought.

37 After this man rose up Judas of Galilee in the days of the taxing, and drew away much people after him: he also perished; and all, even as many as obeyed him, were dispersed.

38 And now I say unto you, Refrain from these men, and let them alone: for if this counsel or this work be of men, it will come to nought:

39 But if it be of God, ye cannot overthrow it; lest haply ye be found even to fight against God.

Gamaliel argued that if the apostles' doctrine was man based, the end would soon come. Conversely, if the Gospel was from God, to act in opposition would be fruitless and would pit the Sanhedrin against God's will. This impeccable reasoning was accepted by the Sanhedrin, even though the apostles were later beaten. After their release, the apostles rejoiced that they "were counted worthy to suffer shame for his name" (Acts 5:41). And Acts 5:42 notes the rest of the story: "And daily in the temple, and in every house, they ceased not to teach and preach Jesus Christ."

My journey is relevant to coming Unexpected Generation members. Those young leaders will challenge conditions and methods found in our churches. If those young leaders employ wisdom similar to Gamaliel's, don't expect everyone to follow quite as easily as the Sanhedrin did. Eliminating mindless rules or balancing worship services to consider members of all age groups will almost always be controversial and divisive, and Unexpected Generation members will, without question, confront ineffective convention. If we realize that God-driven changes will prosper, there is little reason to be apprehensive. If God's will is not present in those changes, time and attendance will tell the story. We may fear that change will lead to diminished attendance and church disputes, but should we not also be in great fear of displeasing God? Is it possible to fight among ourselves and with God too? I can't imagine a more forlorn place to be. Consider Christ's warnings contained in Matthew 15:9–14.

9 But in vain they do worship me, teaching for doctrines the commandments of men.

10 And he called the multitude, and said unto them, Hear, and understand:

11 Not that which goeth into the mouth defileth a man; but that which cometh out of the mouth, this defileth a man.

12 Then came his disciples, and said unto him, Knowest thou that the Pharisees were offended, after they heard this saying?

13 But he answered and said, Every plant, which my heavenly Father hath not planted, shall be rooted up.

14 Let them alone: they be blind leaders of the blind. And if the blind lead the blind, both shall fall into the ditch.

No one wants their lives or church to be uprooted or fall into a ditch. If we love one another and trust God's direction, then we fully and miraculously understand that not all are called in the same manner and that spiritual freedom is not to be feared but rather embraced. The calling of Unexpected Generation members then makes sense. To ignore God's very different calls in different lives stifles the movement of the Holy Spirit and causes divisions over Bible versions, music, missions, and even age groups. Whether we are in church or at the workplace, we all have different roles, levels of performance, and journeys. Like Unexpected

Generation members who will soon follow, I began to question why we attempt to make all of our institutions so uniform. People are different. Needs are different. Communities are different. Churches are different because members are different. Yet many churches seek to copy one another in format, music, and message. Denominational pressures tend to force one size to fit all.

No doubt, some of you reading this brief writing are questioning, searching, and in great need of refreshing your faith. Some of you are churchgoers, and my story frightens you. You do not want to face challenges or ridicule, but you simultaneously realize that something in your place of worship must change. Many Unexpected Generation members are faithful but, to be brutally honest, they despise traditions and definitions that have little to do with true worship and service to God. Religious bureaucracy is as reprehensible as political parties. Shallow commitments and hypocrisy will certainly be questioned by Unexpected Generation members. Consider the following questions that Unexpected Generation members will have no hesitation or reservation asking.

ANNOYING QUESTIONS DIRECTED TO
RELIGIOUS ORGANIZATIONS

Has tradition alienated generations from attending church? Have beliefs been dumbed and watered down to attract people to church? Have churches seeking numbers and inclusion lost their path and members? Has "political correctness" changed the message? Does social justice reconcile with proper doctrine? Did churches just adapt their messages to the social climate? Is that not disastrous and inconsistent? Who let that happen? Is it time for a new Martin Luther? If so, who will take on that role? Who is courageous enough? Smart enough?

Why do church members show up in droves after terrorist attacks or unsettling events? According to a recent report entitled "Georgia

Baptist Convention 2020 Report," updated in 2011 (used with express permission), 70 percent of the population in my home state of Georgia, a Bible Belt state, are lost and unaffected by church and faith. Is that report card acceptable? Are churches becoming less important to society and society less affected and guided by religious principles? (Remember the Millennials?) When did worship become irrelevant to most? Why do we not understand "lostness" and the dwindling influence of organized religion upon society? Does that lack of religious influence affect our character and integrity?

Is *judgment* too harsh a term to share with most church attendees? Do we utilize "grace" as an excuse for ungodly actions? Are we not accountable?

Have our churches taught core beliefs to anyone? Is Christ at the core? Does the Holy Spirit mean anything to a modern world?

Why do some children who were brought up in a religious environment abandon their faith in college? Why is our opportunity to reach young people essentially over after their middle school years? Why does that condition not frighten us? Motivate us? Condemn us? Why do others abandon years of spiritual teaching at the first sign of peer pressure? How effective is our spiritual teaching and preparation? Why do our spiritual principles often fall when we are questioned or we do not fit in? Why are we ashamed of our faith? Can we handle being different?

How do we really feel about those who are different in appearance or live a different lifestyle? Do not their souls matter too? Are we quick to judge and exclude? Is peer pressure ever really over? Is faith as we know it now chasing those in need away?

Are our paths governed by faith, trust, and Scriptures or by fear, cultism, and what others think?

Why is being Christian stigmatizing? Why do liberal media members constantly attack Christianity? What do you think when you hear "born-again Christian"? What about the term *evangelical*?

What reaction do you have to those of other faiths? Are you tolerant? What does your faith say about tolerance?

How many needy people has your church or place of worship served during the last month? If none, why are you there?

Are you really committed to anything spiritual? How is that working for you?

Do denominations matter? Will those denominations survive the emergence of new, young leaders who challenge everything? Are some denominations known by what they are against rather than what they are for?

Remember the rich young ruler found in Luke 18:18–23?

18 And a certain ruler asked him, saying, Good Master, what shall I do to inherit eternal life?

19 And Jesus said unto him, Why callest thou me good? None is good, save one, that is, God.

20 Thou knowest the commandments, Do not commit adultery, Do not kill, Do not steal, Do not bear false witness, Honour thy father and thy mother.

21 And he said, All these have I kept from my youth up.

22 Now when Jesus heard these things, he said unto him, Yet lackest thou one thing: sell all that thou hast, and distribute unto the poor, and thou shalt have treasure in heaven: and come, follow me.

23 And when he heard this, he was very sorrowful: for he was very rich.

If our churches sold all to give to the poor, what would happen? Would the church as we define it cease to exist? Do buildings define the modern church? Is it possible to do with less and then do more?

Is anonymity possible in large congregations? Does anonymity encourage an uncommitted relationship with Christ?

When did churches allow government to take over helping the poor and needy? Is that acceptable?

Why did the baby boomer generation leave the church in droves and take their children with them? What social and financial cost did we experience as a result of this massive abandonment of the church?

Is there a risk that no one will be left to turn the lights off? Is the United States of America necessary to carry the Gospel of Jesus Christ to the world? Have we been preserved only to share the Gospel?

Are we angry at the church? Are we angry with God?

Who will stand for children, for families, and for God? Who will be bold and unashamed of their beliefs? Who believes that good and evil and right and wrong do exist? Who believes that there are contemporary and eternal consequences to our actions?

How will revolutionary young leaders fit into our churches? Will we use them for a convenient season and then abandon them? Do you believe members of the Unexpected Generation have a spiritual reason for being here? Are there any in your place of worship? Have you identified them? Do you believe a small group of spiritually and destiny-driven young people will be able to alter the course of our nation and our institutions, especially the church? Will they be welcomed, or must they establish their own worship methods?

Are the teachings of Jesus welcomed in your church? If so, how do you address, "You must be born again"? Does that message frighten you? How have you personally responded?

Are you a member of a healthy church? How do you define *healthy*?

Are churches relevant to a nation in trouble? Are we truly the body of Christ? Are we honoring his name? How will we be judged by those who follow?

Most important, how will we be judged by our heavenly Father?

CHAPTER 11

Who Is Really to Blame?

We have met the enemy and he is us.
—Pogo

A few years ago, an elderly man visited my law office. He had recently lost his wife and was struggling. Humble, kind, and naïve, he had, I quickly determined, sent a significant amount of money to scam artists who had promised that his prize would be delivered any at moment. You have heard the story before. These scam artists were brazen enough to provide their phone numbers and addresses. No one was threatening to end their activity. These crooks were roaming at will.

Nothing makes me angrier than someone hurting children or old folks. I tracked these crooks down, summarized their activity, and then called the Postal Inspector to see what could be done. I was given a confusing menu of options, none of which included talking to a live person to report a crime. I could fill out a form and wait. That was about it. I tried other federal agencies and got little help or direction. Of course, I was encouraged to contact local officials or make a written report, but I determined that there was neither manpower nor interest in pursuing crooks that preyed on the elderly and naïve. The scammer problem was seemingly just too big and frustrating to address. The crooks in our case were international, some just over the Canadian border, and, of course, that poses problems. If we are incapable or unmotivated to protect our citizens from bold crooks, then what else had slipped through? Terrorists? Mobsters? Human traffickers?

Budgets, manpower, and concerns about broader impact are all in play, I know, but what had happened to this older man was not right, and no one was going to make it right. Contemplating this situation, I began to wonder if our nation was being sacked much like Ancient Rome. Are crooks the new versions of Vandals and Visigoths? If we cannot protect our citizens, what follows?

On the other hand, should I expect my national government to offer protection to a little old man scammed by Canadian crooks? Perhaps this really is a local police matter. Perhaps no government should be involved at all. Maybe we should simply educate our citizenry about crooks. I then questioned, if we ask for less from government, does it oddly and counterintuitively evolve into better government? In other words, if we cut out many of the tasks assigned to government, will the remaining tasks be better performed? Will government save money, become more efficient, and actually provide better basic services? Will we then become more self-reliant and more personally responsible?

Life happens. Things go right; things go wrong. Sickness, death, crooks, financial problems, and disappointments abound. No entity, government, church, or business will ever change that circumstance regardless of how much it tries, spends, or wishes.

My first thought to call someone in government to help with my elderly client's difficulty changes when I redefine the proper role of government. I then ask what I could do or what the client could do to change his circumstance. I would love to confront those crooks, sue them, and pursue them, but economics over a few hundred dollars of loss do not justify those efforts. Government in this instance was correct in being inaccessible and essentially disinterested in my client's problem. Some wrongs are never righted on this side of life. Personal responsibility requires that we take an active role in taking care of our families, the elderly, and the vulnerable. Personal responsibility also dictates that sometimes we just take it on the chin and move on. That is exactly what happened with my client. He moved on with the newfound knowledge that he should check with me before mailing any checks to crooks.

When one declares independence from government's role as our "go to" to address so many of our problems, benefits are immediate and profound. Our mindset changes, Congress changes, economics change, and opportunities change. Less government allows more independence, more personal responsibility, less regulation, less preference for those capable of lobbying or voting in bloc, less societal disruption, more competition, more equality, more liberty, and greater freedom to pursue happiness.

How long has it been since you read the following excerpt:

DECLARATION OF INDEPENDENCE
[Adopted in Congress 4 July 1776]

The Unanimous Declaration of the Thirteen United States of America

When, in the course of human events, it becomes necessary for one people to dissolve the political bands which have connected them with another, and to assume among the powers of the earth, the separate and equal station to which the laws of nature and of nature's God entitle them, a decent respect to the opinions of mankind requires that they should declare the causes which impel them to the separation.

We hold these truths to be self-evident, that all men are created equal, that they are endowed by their Creator with certain unalienable rights, that among these are life, liberty and the pursuit of happiness. That to secure these rights, governments are instituted among men, deriving their just powers from the consent of the governed. That whenever any form of government becomes destructive to these ends, it is the right of the people to alter or to abolish it, and to institute new government, laying its foundation on such principles and organizing its powers in such form, as to them shall seem most likely to effect their safety and happiness. Prudence, indeed, will dictate that governments long established should not be changed for light and transient causes; and accordingly all experience hath shown that mankind are more disposed to suffer, while evils are sufferable, than to right themselves by abolishing the forms to which they are accustomed. But when a long train of abuses and usurpations, pursuing invariably the same object evinces a design to reduce them under absolute despotism, it is their right, it is their duty, to throw off such government, and to provide new guards for their future security....

And for the support of this declaration, with a firm reliance on the protection of Divine Providence, we mutually pledge to each other our lives, our fortunes and our sacred honor.

Unexpected Generation members understand this living document. They will question the oppressiveness of our own expectations and the distorted version of government we have come to expect.

ANNOYING QUESTIONS DIRECTED AT GOVERNMENT

Is it time to "throw off such government" and in the process throw off our own expectations? Are Unexpected Generation members the new guards of "future security"? Do we have any "sacred honor" left? Do we even know what honor is?

Why did we ever look to government as our problem solver? When did deficits ever make sense? Does anyone in government ever listen? Do we have a voice as a people, or are we so distracted, diffused, and overwhelmed that no clear voice is possible? Are only the loudest heard by those in power? What about voices with money behind them? Does your vote matter?

Is it not possible to retire our national debt in a generation? Is it not possible to stop spending more than we take in? Is it not appropriate for state governments to replace most functions of federal government? Does anyone in Congress think we can handle the truth? Do they think we are that stupid?

Does Congress or any legislature need to meet so often? Why? Do we need any new laws? Don't we have enough already? What about retiring some old laws? Why not less rather than more? Do we just pass new laws to enhance reelection for politicians and build their reputations? Should there be short term limits for all members of Congress? Wouldn't it be wise to remove everyone from office and start over? Why do those in power seek to stay in power? Why not pass the torch to others? Why do so many of our best people avoid running for office? Why would a decent man or woman ever expose his or her family to hateful scrutiny in a political campaign? Why do we need to know every detail of their lives? Do I really care about their net worth or which company they hold stock in? Should we be more interested in ideas, character, and generational concern? *Why have statesmen been replaced by statists?*

How many in government wish to silence you? Jail you? Destroy your family? Destroy your business? Your place of worship? How many in government stand for truth, free speech, and more freedoms? How many elected officials care about anything but their careers?

Are you ever excited about ideas, about liberty, about casting off those restraints that government imposes on our lives? Are you responsible with your freedoms?

Is there ever a need for governmental preferences? Affirmative action? Should race, sex, religion, or national origin ever be a criterion to prefer one citizen over another? Are we not beyond that now? Is government, in preferring one group over another, not biased, racist, and divisional? When should that circumstance end? Was it ever really necessary? Are those programs punitive? Was that the intent?

When did our government become enamored with socialism? Why does our tax structure punish achievement? Why do tax policies include any agenda other than the creation of revenue? Why should any function of government have a purpose other than the protection of its citizens? And if that protection is not equally applied, is that policy or agenda proper?

Why is government hostile to businesses? Families? Who decides the agenda? Why are those agendas taught in our schools?

When do entitlement payments crush our government and potentially our economy? What happens when those payments cannot be made? Has government prepared for that eventuality?

Will government seek to destroy the Unexpected Generation? Who will you stand with?

What is your declaration? Is it one of independence or dependence? Does not government mimic God with its distance, power, and provision? Is that a form of idolatry? *Is your future founded in God or government?* Your answer has eternal consequences.

CHAPTER 12

Finally, Some Answers

"Never, never, never, never give up."
—Winston Churchill

My grandmother occasionally prepared cinnamon rolls from leftover biscuit dough. Those cinnamon rolls, loaded with butter and sugar, were outrageously good. (I did not say *healthy*.) Noting her grandchildren's delight and excitement over this special treat, just for fun, she named her culinary masterpiece "toad frogs." Grandmother shared freely, so it was not unusual for her to offer lunch to anyone around at the proper hour. A telephone repairman just happened to be in her home on a day when those wonderful cinnamon rolls were prepared. As she removed them from the oven, Grandmother asked the repairman if he would like a hot "toad frog"? "Ma'am, I am not sure," he replied, obviously not all that interested in an amphibian snack. She sensed his confusion and identified the cinnamon rolls as the toad frogs, and they both enjoyed a cinnamon roll and a good laugh.

Questions, properly answered, may result in tasty treats or the delicious prospect of restoration. Old time revival meetings usually posed questions such as, "Are you ready?" and "Are you prepared?" Those are fair questions for our time.

Throughout this writing, certain questions were marked in italics to provide a "bread crumb trail" to some the most important questions of our time. Those questions are listed below:

- Do we really believe that America is somehow exempt from the aftermath of poor stewardship?
- Do we have a destiny of prosperity and blessings regardless of our actions and beliefs?
- Is there an end?
- What happened?
- Is not the storm where Christians thrive, serve, and share a peace that the world does not understand?
- Are we really exceptional or just riding along on past successes?
- Could we as a nation be better, do better, be freer?
- How will one of the most diverse generations in the history of the nation coalesce into conservatism, reform, and renewal?
- Do we not hide behind wrong questions and answers?
- God, what may I do for you?
- Is any idea, any thought, any concept more important than you and your family?
- Are you talking a good game or playing one?
- Does "moral" matter?
- Are we truly ready for the "next level"?
- Are our paths governed by faith, trust, and Scriptures or by fear, cultism, and what others think?
- Are churches relevant to a nation in trouble?
- Why have statesmen been replaced by statists?
- Is your future founded in God or government?

I could say that those are questions, among many others, that must be answered. But I won't. I won't say that because Unexpected Generation members will offer answers to these questions and will add others, including, How do we restore our nation and its people? How do we become stronger in our service to God? How do we define good leadership? and How do we accept the benefits of personal responsibility? Those leaders are coming, and their annoying questions are coming with them. The season of denial and dodging tough questions and answers is almost over. Thank God!

Expect excitement as parents and grandparents serve alongside their descendants. Those too young to serve will be aware that history is being made. Imagine the admiration for a big brother or big sister or someone from the neighborhood who commits all to save our land. Those preferring our current course will resist those efforts and sacrifices, but that resistance will ultimately fail. Correction and course changes are not always pleasant, and long-delayed course changes make remedies that much more difficult.

Unexpected Generation members are prepared for difficulty, but they will need encouragement, safe places to live, our support, and our prayers. Those leaders will buffer us from extreme violence and the utter destruction of our nation that would have been our future without God's intervention. God's intervention has already occurred with the birth and preparation of our coming leaders. Our survival, our freedoms, and our dreams will soon be in the hands of a relatively small group of patriots. Many grew up watching *The Patriot, Braveheart,* and *Independence Day,* movies that captured their imaginations and inspired their belief that this country is worth the fight. Recently *The Hunger Games,* captured this group's imagination. God's call in their lives is, no doubt, most important.

Some emerging leaders have delayed having families, somehow knowing that the next few years will be challenging. Many are in our military. Many are in church youth groups. Many are charismatic leaders in arenas ranging from business to education. These leaders believe in a future of amazingly advanced technology existing simultaneously with values and a work ethic of a bygone era.

Are you ready for instability? Economic uncertainty? Possible collapse of our national government? Do you realize that evil will attempt to seize power at every opportunity? Are you able to discern differences between Unexpected Generation members and warlords?

You have surely added your own questions. You may never see a need for an Unexpected Generation and may believe that a big event is unlikely or perhaps inevitable, just not in our lifetimes. You may look at your son or daughter and wonder what his or her role will be and what the future holds. You may feel insecure, worried, or anxious. You also may be very excited. Some of you are impatient and cannot wait for coming change. Some of you hope to die first. I can only offer the assurance that God is in charge and that he loves us. His love always seeks what is best. While we all have our version of what is best, God's "best" sees long term, well into the next generation and beyond. He may carry us close to the abyss, but he absolutely does not ever want us to leave his loving presence. We may choose the wrong answers, and those answers may lead to destruction, but such is never God's will. God vigorously pursues us not for punishment but because he wants a deeper and more meaningful relationship with his children. Remember John 3:16? "For God so loved the world, that he gave his only begotten Son, that whosoever believeth in him should not perish, but have everlasting life."

That love matters. God never quits, and he doesn't like losing either. Luke 19:10 states: "For the Son of man is come to seek and to save that which was lost."

You may have been lost in the deluge of questions offered in this writing. I pray that immersion led to some self-examination and a realization that difficult questions are not deadly but very necessary to understand our future. Our nation is different. We are exceptional and, to some extent, unpredictable. We have experienced unbelievable troubles and trials throughout our history. We have also known grinding despair and fear. Yet God has pursued us and allowed this great nation not only to survive but at one time prosper spiritually and financially. That prosperity is not just a distant memory.

Remarkable pent-up demand currently exists in the United States. A long recession reminds us of how much we like material goods. A poor economy has required many of us to patch up, get by, and make do. Our economy will recover; new items will eventually be required. We will thrive again despite dismal warnings of lowered expectations; families will once again want and need new houses, cars, and dishwashers. For far too long, we have patched up and gotten by with poor leadership, failed policies, and unholy lifestyles. Pent-up demand exists for leadership, for a relationship with God, and for hope and restoration. That hope and restoration will come as we begin answering questions that will and must define our destinies. A long famine is nearing an end. Refreshing rain is beginning to fall.

Perhaps the final and greatest question of all is simply, When does this all start? I can answer that one—soon. Very soon.

Afterword

In 2011, I attended a special Sunday morning worship service to commemorate the tenth anniversary of September 11, 2001. Television shows the evening before reminded me of that horrible day a decade earlier when thousands of precious lives were lost in a moment of madness. I recalled standing outside of my home on the evening of September 11, 2001, vainly trying to make sense of those events. Shivering in the chill of an east wind, I wondered about the winds of war, of what was to come, and how all those events would affect my nation and my family. All I could see that evening were more attacks, wars, and threats. No doubt, we were all scared.

The worship service I attended focused on the following Scripture in Acts (27:20–24):

20 And when neither sun nor stars in many days appeared, and no small tempest lay on [us], all hope that we should be saved was then taken away.

21 But after long abstinence Paul stood forth in the midst of them, and said, Sirs, ye should have hearkened unto me, and not have loosed from Crete, and to have gained this harm and loss.

22 And now I exhort you to be of good cheer: for there shall be no loss of [any man's] life among you, but of the ship.

23 For there stood by me this night the angel of God, whose I am, and whom I serve,

24 Saying, Fear not, Paul; thou must be brought before Caesar: and, lo, God hath given thee all them that sail with thee.

I did not realize that less than ten miles away, the Sunday school that my wife attended used the same scripture at virtually the same time. I considered why this Scripture resonated with a teacher and a preacher on that special day.

For a very long time, we have lived in darkness, in a tempest, and with little hope. Such is the "ship" of our nation. Paul, on his way to his death in Rome, stood first to remind his shipmates that he had told them so, as he had requested the trip be aborted due to weather. Nobody listened. Paul had warned of dangers, and that warning was ignored.

Paul also experienced an angelic message that all would be well. The ship was toast but not those sharing a ride. Note that the storm was large, the heavens obscured, and hope taken away. Those onboard were afraid and resigned to death. Except for Paul, everyone had given up. Paul encouraged, told of his angel encounter, and related his destiny to go to Rome. Those listening probably thought, *Paul, I like what you are saying—except about the ship. You see, we are in the Mediterranean, in a storm with a leaky boat but a boat nonetheless, and you tell us that we are about to lose this last hope we have. How is that good news?*

Is not Paul's experience familiar? Our nation has been in darkness; hope has exited for so many, and the ship is sinking. Warnings have been ignored. How do we symbolically or allegorically define *ship*? Is it our current course as a nation or our nation itself? Is the "ship" our lifestyles or the condition of our churches? What about our economy? Our families? Our traditions? Our hopes and dreams as we define them? Our addictions, our entitlement mentality, our resistance to change? Is it okay if that ship sinks and we are freed from all the worries about the ship leaking, creaking, and groaning?

Even though we are storm tossed right now, God has a marvelous plan not only for our personal salvation but for our nation too. His plans do result in some pretty amazing destinies.

Consider beautiful Queen Esther, who is no doubt a forerunner to our Unexpected Generation members. God's plan for her life afforded beauty, favor, and an opportunity to marry King Xerxes. Her mentor, Mordecai, had prior to that marriage adopted an orphaned cousin, Esther, and reared her as a daughter. His words in Esther 4:13–14 chillingly underscore God's plan not only in Esther's life but for those who follow.

> 13 Then Mordecai commanded to answer Esther, Think not with thyself that thou shalt escape in the king's house, more than all the Jews.
>
> 14 For if thou altogether holdest thy peace at this time, then shall there enlargement and deliverance arise to the Jews from another place; but thou and thy father's house shall be destroyed: and who knoweth whether thou art come to the kingdom for such a time as this?

Mordecai's question forced Esther to make a grave decision. Any failure to answer or act risked not only to her destruction but her people as well. Mordecai challenged Esther to assume her destiny, to know that God prepared her for "such a time as this." This was an incredible moment, a moment when a young woman had the weight of posterity on her shoulders. Esther risked death in approaching King Xerxes with a bold plan to rescue her people. Her courage and spiritual beauty are evident in Esther 4:16, which states, "Go, gather together all the Jews that are present in Shushan, and fast ye for me, and neither eat nor drink three days, night or day: I also and my maidens will fast likewise; and so will I go in unto the king, which is not according to the law: and if I perish, I perish."

Surrendering to God's will, Esther was prepared to sacrifice her life for her people and a cause. Esther's decision affects you today because her people were saved and that salvation was part of God's plan to send our Savior. God had placed Esther in that moment in history to matter, and she did.

Esther is a wonderful example for Unexpected Generation members. She undertook great risk, faced imminent danger, and took a bold stand that, with God's help, saved a nation. She answered a question that Unexpected Generation members must also answer, which is simply whether they have come into the world for such a time as this. Their affirmative answer must be given not according to man's ways and laws but because God has a plan and that plan is so compelling, so powerful, and so ordained in young lives that they will serve regardless of the risk. If they perish, they perish, but without their God-inspired actions, our nation, too, will no doubt perish. Those young people are that important and that timely.

We may have many challenges, but God has prepared not only a Savior who will one day return but also, in the interim, a group of remarkable young people charged with helping restore our nation. I am very thankful for God's provision, and I can't wait for Unexpected Generation members to fulfill their destinies. Your awareness of this coming event is vital, but so is the awareness that our forgiving and loving heavenly Father has an interest in this nation not as a failure or byword but as a shining light carrying the Gospel to our own and to the uttermost parts of the Earth.

And that comment provides an appropriate ending, with the exception of one final question. Will we trust, embrace, become excited about, and enjoy the destiny that God has in store for us? I think you know the answer.

→ "Be strong and of a good courage, fear not, nor be afraid of them: for the LORD thy God, he it is that doth go with thee; he will not fail thee, nor forsake thee" (Deut. 31:6).

God bless.

Works Cited

1. References to Scripture throughout are to the King James Version of the *Holy Bible* unless otherwise noted.

2. Pew Research Center, dated December 11, 2009, "The Millennials" by Scott Keeter and Paul Taylor (http://pewresearch.org/pubs/1437/millenials-profile) (used with express permission), as utilized in Chapter 4 and with subsequent references to Millennials.

3. "Georgia Baptist Convention 2020 Report," updated in 2011 (used with express permission) as utilized in Chapter 10.

NOTES

NOTES

NOTES

About the Author

Author Phill Bettis is a resident of Cumming, Georgia, where he has practiced law for over three decades. He is married to Wanda Lynn (Burruss) Bettis, and they have three adult children. Phill is active in several community and charitable activities. He enjoys traveling, archeology, history, and writing. He has previously contributed articles to the *Forsyth County News* and history-related magazines and publications.

CPSIA information can be obtained at www.ICGtesting.com
Printed in the USA
LVOW040056020113

313915LV00001B/5/P